Event Leadership

Theory and methods for event management and tourism

Emma Abson

With contributions by Miriam Firth and Jane Tattersall

Goodfellow Publishers Ltd

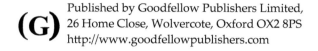
Published by Goodfellow Publishers Limited,
26 Home Close, Wolvercote, Oxford OX2 8PS
http://www.goodfellowpublishers.com

British Library Cataloguing in Publication Data: a catalogue record for this title is available from the British Library.

Library of Congress Catalog Card Number: on file.

ISBN: 978-1-911635-26-0

DOI: 10.23912/9781911635253-4274

The Events Management Theory and Methods Series

Copyright © Emma Abson, 2021

All rights reserved. The text of this publication, or any part thereof, may not be reproduced or transmitted in any form or by any means, electronic or mechanical, including photocopying, recording, storage in an information retrieval system, or otherwise, without prior permission of the publisher or under licence from the Copyright Licensing Agency Limited. Further details of such licences (for reprographic reproduction) may be obtained from the Copyright Licensing Agency Limited, of Saffron House, 6–10 Kirby Street, London EC1N 8TS.

 Design and typesetting by P.K. McBride, www.macbride.org.uk

Cover design by Cylinder

Contents

Introduction to the Events Management Theory and Methods Series	v
Preface	vii
Author biographies	ix

1 What is leadership? — **1**

Introduction	1
A brief review of the historical development of leadership	4
Defining leadership	6
Criticisms of leadership studies	8
Leadership in the event literature	12
The workforce of the future and events careers	14
Leadership in action: Industry insight from Lils Collingwood	16

2 Classic approaches to leadership — **23**

Classic approaches to leadership – entity approaches	23
Behavioural theories of leadership – what do leaders do?	26
Contingency leadership – what leaders do depends on the situation	30
Theory X and Y	33
Event research and leadership style	36
Leadership in action: Industry insight from Jason Allan Scott	38

3 Leader/follower perspectives — **44**

Leader/follower perspectives – entity-relational approaches	44
Charismatic leadership	46
Transactional and transformational leadership	47
Followship in leadership studies	52
Leader-Member Exchange (LMX)	53
Leadership in action: Industry insight from Scott Taylor	57

4 The new wave of leadership studies — **64**

The new wave of moral leadership studies	64
Ethical leadership	65
Authentic leadership	68
Servant leadership	70
Leadership in action: Industry insight from Melissa Noakes	74

5 Leadership as a collective process — **80**

Leadership as a collectivistic process	80
The rise of collective leadership perspectives	82
Shared leadership	84
Team leadership	87
Social identity theories of leadership	89
Leadership in action: Industry insight from Eamonn Hunt	92

6	**Leadership as a skill**	**102**
	Leadership as a skill	102
	Competency based leadership	103
	Specific event competencies	105
	Leadership in action: Industry insight from David Strafford	109
7	**Knowledge and event leadership**	**115**
	Introduction	115
	The value of knowledge	116
	Aspects of knowledge	118
	Aspects of tacit knowledge	122
	Knowledge management	123
	Barriers and challenges	126
	Leadership in action: Knowledge management in small and medium sized enterprises	128
8	**Events, leadership and power**	**136**
	Introduction	136
	Who leads, and when – and what does that have to do with power?	137
	The power of leadership	138
	Access to leadership = access to power	141
	The power of events and event communities	142
	Stakeholder management, leadership and power	145
	Leadership in action: Industry insight from Carrie Abernathy	147
9	**Modelling events as social agents of change**	**151**
	Introduction	151
	Social agents of change: A definition	152
	Events as SACs	156
	Events are a stage	158
	Events are mirrors of society	161
	Events can be leaderless	163
	Events lead to new employment practices	165
	Leadership in action: Industry insight from Rose Wilcox	167
	Index	**175**

Introduction to the Events Management Theory and Methods Series

Event management as a field of study and professional practice has its textbooks with plenty of models and advice, a body of knowledge (EMBOK), competency standards (MBECS) and professional associations with their codes of conduct. But to what extent is it truly an applied management field? In other words, where is the management theory in event management, how is it being used, and what are the practical applications?

Event tourism is a related field, one that is defined by the roles events play in tourism and economic development. The primary consideration has always been economic, although increasingly events and managed event portfolios meet more diverse goals for cities and countries. While the economic aspects have been well developed, especially economic impact assessment and forecasting, the application of management theory to event tourism has not received adequate attention.

In this book series we launch a process of examining the extent to which mainstream theory is being employed to develop event-specific theory, and to influence the practice of event management and event tourism. This is a very big task, as there are numerous possible theories, models and concepts, and virtually unlimited advice available on the management of firms, small and family businesses, government agencies and not-for-profits. Inevitably, we will have to be selective.

The starting point is theory. Scientific theory must both explain a phenomenon, and be able to predict what will happen. Experiments are the dominant form of classical theory development. But for management, predictive capabilities are usually lacking; it might be wiser to speak of theory in development, or theory fragments. It is often the process of theory development that marks research in management, including the testing of hypotheses and the formulation of propositions. Models, frameworks, concepts and sets of propositions are all part of this development.

The following diagram illustrates this approach. All knowledge creation has potential application to management, as does theory from any discipline or field. The critical factor for this series is how the theory and related methods can be applied. In the core of this diagram are management and business theories which are the most directly pertinent, and they are often derived from foundation disciplines.

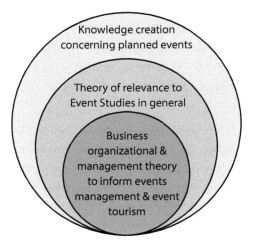

All the books in this series will be relatively short, and similarly structured. They are designed to be used by teachers who need theoretical foundations and case studies for their classes, by students in need of reference works, by professionals wanting increased understanding alongside practical methods, and by agencies or associations that want their members and stakeholders to have access to a library of valuable resources. The nature of the series is that as it grows, components can be assembled by request. That is, users can order a book or collection of chapters to exactly suit their needs.

All the books will introduce the theory, show how it is being used in the events sector through a literature review, incorporate examples and case studies written by researchers and/or practitioners, and contain methods that can be used effectively in the real world.

Preface

Key objectives of the book

- ☐ Inform readers of leadership theory and practice for events and event tourism, including key concepts and definitions
- ☐ Discuss key leadership challenges for events and event tourism
- ☐ Examine the role of 'the leader' within event organisations
- ☐ Explore leadership in a range of event settings
- ☐ Develop professionalism for leadership in these fields
- ☐ Examine the role that event leadership plays in society
- ☐ Examine the role of events as catalysts for social and cultural change
- ☐ Recommend the relevant leadership behaviours and theories
- ☐ Connect readers to the relevant research literature.

A lack of research into human resource development, managerial skillsets and leadership practices of event managers has meant that there is very little understanding of the contribution that leadership makes to the management of experiences. The purpose of this book is to shine a light on leadership theory and explore how it relates to the unique context of planned events and event tourism. An understanding of leadership is essential for the development of successful event managers and for the delivery of successful event experiences – whilst some sectors of the leisure industry are run by large corporations, with well-established leadership structures in place, the event industry tends to be more transient, and often has temporary management structures which exist only for the duration of the event. In addition, the difference in leadership required for a small-scale local community event and that of a large-scale international event such as Glastonbury Festival is vast. This is the tension at the heart of leadership within events – event projects are intangible and temporary in nature and they provide only one opportunity to get it right. However, in order for event managers to be successful leaders, they also need to work in teams, motivating, empowering and developing team members. This is the challenge in planned events and makes them a unique context within which to study leadership.

This book explores the key questions of how those who work in events resolve the tension between the intangibility of event experiences, the planned nature of the events, and how event managers become successful leaders and lead successful event experiences. The purpose of this book is therefore to provide a concise introduction to leadership theory and methods for use in event management and event tourism.

How to use this book

Each chapter begins with a set of learning objectives which describe the key focus of that chapter. Each of the learning objectives suggests one or more study or discussion questions, as the reader should be able to demonstrate the applicable knowledge drawn from the chapter. Further questions that could be integrated into study can be found at the end of the chapter, along with further reading suggestions – these are typically 3-5 additional texts which the authors believe will help to develop understanding of key topics further. Each chapter also has a 'voice from the event industry' at the end of it – these industry insights enable the reader to gain useful insights into how leadership works in the event industry. Lastly, each chapter has an introduction and summary which highlights the key areas discussed in the body of the chapter.

Acknowledgements

This book would not have been made possible without the wonderful support of the two contributors Jane Tattersall and Miriam Firth. Their contributions and expertise (in Chapters 7 and 9) have added value and insight to this book, that was far beyond my own area of knowledge. I am also extremely grateful to those wonderful people from industry – Melissa, Scott, Carrie, Lils, Jason, David, Rose and Eamonn – who, despite the most challenging of years, still managed to find the time to pen thoughtful, insightful and illuminating insights that support each of the chapters. Without these insights from the event industry, the book would be less rich, and less useful to the readers.

I am also, of course, grateful to my colleagues and to my family for allowing me to carve out the time to write this book – in particular, to Andrew, who helped with the proof reading (so I can now blame any mistakes on him…!) Lastly, I am thankful to the staff at Goodfellow and to Professor Don Getz for all their support.

Author biographies

Dr Emma Abson

Emma is a Senior Lecturer at Sheffield Hallam University. She teaches across a number of postgraduate and undergraduate modules, as well as being an active researcher. Her research focuses on leadership in organisations and in teams, and her PhD focused on leadership in events. Emma has co-authored a leading textbook on Events Management, published a number of articles in academic journals and sits on the editorial board of the *Events Management Journal*. Prior to becoming an academic, Emma had a successful career in the events industry, most notably as a head of department leading on a wide range of business to business and corporate events.

Dr Miriam Firth

Miriam is a Senior Lecturer at the University of Manchester, UK. Her research interests include vocational education and training, employability, intercultural training and management, and event leadership.

Jane Tattersall

Jane is a Principal Lecturer and Subject Group Leader for the Events Management courses at Sheffield Hallam University, teaching across a range of modules, specialising in event design and delivery. Jane's research interest is in tacit knowledge management in music festivals and strategic event design. Prior to joining the University she had 20 years commercial and non profit events industry experience and still very much enjoys current roles at music festivals during summers, as on-site volunteer manager and community liaison manager.

Event Leadership

1 What is leadership?

Chapter aims

- ☐ Introduce the historical development of leadership studies
- ☐ Understand the various definitions of leadership
- ☐ Critically discuss the difference between leadership and management
- ☐ Explore why leadership differs in events and event tourism to other areas of management
- ☐ Learn why leadership matters in professional practice
- ☐ Focus on leadership in action: how to get a job leading events – industry insight from Lils Collingwood, Albany Appointments.

Introduction

Nearly 100 years of leadership studies have resulted in a large body of literature that suggests that leadership matters in all aspects of life. Studies have also shown that soft skills, such as leadership, are key to continued success in complex, fast changing organisations, and in a variety of managerial contexts. The nature of leadership within organisations and the styles of leadership required for specific business management roles have frequently been studied and there is a broad consensus that leadership matters in a range of managerial positions including event project management, tourism and hospitality management, human resources and a variety of other senior organisational roles. Leadership practices are essential for the development of successful event managers and leadership in planned events and event tourism therefore cannot be ignored.

Once you understand the basics as described in this book, you should be able to identify and classify a variety of event leadership practices. You should also be able to identify how leadership is enacted in event and event tourism organisations. This chapter starts with basic definitions, then goes on to fully explore why leadership matters in events and event tourism.

To get the reader thinking about leadership in planned events and event tourism, consider these scenarios:

1 The event manager for a large, international festival has complete control of the project plan, delegates all the work to her large team herself and is the key point of contact for all the major stakeholders. She is taken seriously and suddenly ill two weeks before the event is due to take place. What happens to the festival if the person with all that essential knowledge is suddenly not available to run it?

2 An experiential event agency is working with a large corporation on its experiential marketing, but the client is very fussy and the lead contact is a very difficult person to deal with, disagreeing with everything the agency suggests. How does the agency lead a project in this environment?

3 A human resource department has been asked to produce some leadership training for the recent event management graduate recruits. What kind of training would they need to develop? What skills might be useful for these new event leaders?

4 An event organisation is owned and run by the entrepreneurial founder of the business. The business has done very well in the past, but the owner is very controlling, and insists each decision is run past him before it can be made. This slows down the team's ability to respond to clients' queries and makes quick decision making and problem solving impossible. In addition, this man holds all the power and he has a very bad temper, so everyone in the organisation is scared of him, and can't challenge the status quo. What impact will this have on the team's ability to deliver events?

5 A destination marketing organisation (DMO) is developing an event portfolio for a small city. The city has suffered from a very poor reputation in recent years, with high levels of crime and poverty. How can the DMO use the event portfolio to lead changes to the perception of the city?

In the first example, the risk is obvious – when only one person fully understands the operational processes of an event, then both the responsibility and the knowledge sits firmly with them. If that person becomes suddenly unavailable, then the whole event is at risk. Good leadership would solve this because good leadership involves the delegation of responsibility and the development of trust in your team to manage the necessary tasks. Good leaders spread leadership throughout their organisations, and throughout their teams – both to lessen the risk of jeopardising the event, and to motivate and empower their staff members. An empowered, motivated team means a happy team – and therefore a team that will deliver the best experience they can. Types of leadership that might support this empowerment are discussed in Chapters 3, 4 and 5, and issues around knowledge are explored in Chapter 7.

The second example is more complex and leads us to ask questions about who leads and when. Is the client or the agency a leader in this scenario? The answer is that they should both lead at appropriate times, and both parties should be willing to accept leadership from the other. The client has specialist knowledge of their brand, product and customer. The agency has specialist knowledge of events and event experiences – if they both listen to each other and accept leadership from those with expertise, then the project will go well. However, in circumstances such as the one described here, how likely is it that the client contact will listen and accept that he might be making poor decisions? A different type of leadership is required, one in which the client feels in control and the agency is there to 'serve' – this is explored in Chapter 4.

The third scenario is perhaps the most complex of them all – how do you train people in leadership, when leadership must change all the time, depending on who and what you are leading. Currently, most training still boils down to leadership styles and leadership competencies. These are explored in Chapter 6 – but the reader is encouraged to remember that leadership should be adaptable and how it is enacted should change depending on the situation in which it is taking place. In addition, remember that events are all about relationships. Understanding how to lead those relationships is not only a key skill needed for event managers, but will facilitate better event experiences. This is explored throughout this book.

The fourth example suggests an autocratic leader – perhaps someone who considers himself to be a 'great man'. This type of leadership – explored in Chapter 2 – is difficult to deal with, as these leaders are sure they are always right, insists that employees do as they say and rarely accept advice from others. It is not always pleasant to work with people who exhibit this type of leadership. But that is not to say that there is no place for it – at certain points in an event cycle, when the risk is high and quick decision making is crucial, having a decisive and controlling person in charge can help to keep the event from collapsing in on itself. There is a time for all sorts of leadership – the best event leaders will adopt the right type of leadership at the right time.

The last scenario challenges us to think about leadership from a different perspective – not as something someone does, or as a process that people can participate in. Instead, we are asking you here to consider events as thought leaders – the event experience itself can educate communities, it can modify behaviours and it can create long lasting memories. The power of events as influencers within society and their ability to act as catalysts for change should not be overlooked. In Chapters 8 and 9, we explore how event leadership is more than how to be a good leader – it is also about events that shape the future in politics, society and the economy.

All these scenarios suggest the same conclusion – managing events is no longer enough; we now need event leadership. And understanding leadership theory is the key to current event students becoming future event leaders.

A brief review of the historical development of leadership

The study of leadership spans over 100 years and now consists of a vast body of literature that demonstrates a wide range of evolving views on the nature of human behaviour and how people acquire, develop and practice leadership (Avolio, Walumbwa, & Weber, 2009). Each decade brings a raft of new theories, models and frameworks and a range of criticisms of that which has gone before. This book does not have the capacity to cover all of the theoretical developments within leadership studies, so instead, we will highlight the dominant discourses that exist within leadership studies and examine why this matters in the context of planned events and event tourism.

There have been several significant shifts in scholarly approaches to leadership – these shifts can be summarised as a move from focussing upon who the individual is (e.g. trait theories) to looking at what the individual does (e.g. behavioural theories) and the context they do it in (e.g. situational context theories) and the competencies needed to lead (the competency school of leadership). These approaches to understanding leadership all share the view that leadership is a specialised role – they focus on the individual and, whilst some of these theories looked at what other influences there may be (i.e. followers, or situational context), they do so through the lens of the primary leader, carrying out leadership functions. Recently however, this view of leadership has faced increasing criticism as scholars have begun to reject the idea that one person can have a significant impact on an entire organisation. Instead, scholars have begun to focus on the relational aspects of leadership, as scholars consider how interpersonal relationships inform leadership practice. In this school of leadership thought, scholars focus particularly on the influential aspects of leadership (e.g. charismatic leadership, transformational leadership and leader-member exchange theories).

Lastly, there is something of a 'new wave' emerging within leadership studies, which represents a diversification of thinking around how leadership occurs, and what leadership actually is. Badaracco (2001) describes this as a 'post-heroic' phase – and this represents a significant shift in leadership theory. For example, in recent years, a number of very public corporate scandals (such as Enron and Lehmann Brothers) have created an interest on ethical and moral behaviours of leaders. This has resulted in three emerging forms of 'positive' leadership studies – authentic leadership, ethical leadership and servant leadership, sometimes described as theories of the 'new hero' (Yammarino, 2013). These 'positive' forms of leadership focus on leader behaviours that are ethical, moral, professional and socially responsible, and suggest that the leader's interpersonal dynamics will increase the followers' confidence and motivate them to perform better than is expected. Authentic, ethical and servant leadership perspectives are conceptually closely related both to each other, and to the field of transformational leadership. Later developments of these theories suggest that transformational leaders can also be unethical, abusive, or self-serving (think, if you like, of the 45th president of the United States here). Another set of emerging leadership theory can be described as collective leadership – in this, scholars consider that leadership is not just found in the role of the formal leader, but is also found in the interaction of team members to lead the team by sharing leadership responsibilities. There is then a growing body of research that convincingly argues that leadership is relational and multi-level, which involves leaders, followers, and the social influence processes of larger networks (e.g. shared or distributed leadership).

Defining leadership

Whilst most scholars agree that leadership matters, many suggest that there is a vagueness and uncertainly around what leadership is. There exists no agreement on a universal definition of leadership, and each school of thought offers their own views and specific definitions of what they mean by leadership. These can be summarised as:

♦ Leadership is a trait or an ability – Chapter 2

♦ Leadership is a behaviour – Chapters 2 and 3

♦ Leadership is a relationship – Chapter 3 and 4

♦ Leadership is a skill or a competency –Chapter 6

♦ Leadership is an influence process – Chapters 3, 4 and 5

Each of these differing views will be discussed in the relevant chapters of this book. It is, however, important that readers of this book understand how I have come to my understanding of leadership – the hope here is that ambiguity on what I mean by leadership will be removed by the provision of a clear definition.

This book therefore adopts Yukl (2010) definition of leadership – *"Leadership is the process of influencing others to understand and agree about what needs to be done and how to do it, and the process of facilitating individual and collective efforts to accomplish shared objectives"* (p.8). This position acknowledges that trying to answer the question 'what is leadership?' is an impossible endeavour, as the answer is constantly revised as people interact with a variety of leaders and their experience of leadership changes.

Simply put, leadership means something different to every person, and even their own interpretations will shift over time, or in different contexts. This book therefore discusses leadership in a broad sense, as an influence process that resides in relationships. That said, it is necessary to understand and be able to apply the full range of scholarly definitions of leadership – which is why this book includes sections on leadership traits, leadership behaviours and leadership competencies. How you decide to interpret what leadership means, and what good leadership is, will be up to you.

What leadership is not: Leadership and management

Most leadership texts differentiate between leadership and management, but in reality the terms are often used interchangeably. And they can be quite similar. Both leaders and managers are involved in the management of people, in arranging resources and motivating people. The difference can be seen in that managers plan to maintain order and organise the necessary resources, whereas leaders establish the direction of the business or the team. Leaders motivate, inspire and empower. Managers control, problem solve and maintain order (Kotterman, 2006).

This doesn't mean that managers are not leaders, and leaders do not manage. In fact many people are leader-managers – responsible for both the day to day running of their teams or departments, and also for inspiring and motivating employees to get the best out of them. In events, however, is not unusual for people to over-manage and under-lead – too much time spent on the project management, without enough consideration to leading the vision of the event, or aligning the organisations goals with the planned experience. There is a strong argument for leadership and management to be separated out and considered as two distinct tasks. Nearly every event employee will manage aspects of the event, but they will also have the opportunity to lead at some point, and given the transient, instantaneous nature of event delivery, they must do so well.

> Interested in reading more about the difference between leadership and management? See Kotterman (2006), in the recommended reading.

Criticisms of leadership studies

It is important to start this book with a holistic view of discussions around leadership – as such a brief discussion on those that criticise the study of leadership is necessary.

So vast is the field of leadership studies that some scholars have begun to question if the proliferation of leadership theories is warranted, considering the lack of evidence that each theory is substantively different from those that have gone before it (e.g. Banks, Gooty, Ross, Williams, & Harrington, 2018). A criticism often aimed at leadership studies is the underlying assumption that leadership exists as distinct phenomenon and that leadership matters. These assumptions have always run alongside the rhetoric of leadership, with little critical questioning (Alvesson & Spicer, 2012). Viewing leadership as distinct from other behaviours, competencies or traits is problematic because *"leadership actually refers to an unwieldy bundle of apparently unrelated activities"* (Alvesson & Spicer, 2012, p. 317) and this 'bundle' cannot be measured as an isolated phenomenon. If we agree that leadership is complex, then any research findings that fail to address this complexity are at best ambiguous and at worst completely irrelevant (Yukl, 2010). In the extremity of these criticisms, scholars like Calder (1977) have suggested that leadership exists only in the ideas of others and therefore cannot be considered a scientific construct that is worthy of study.

However, in order to make some sense of the literature to date, I will suggest, as others have before me, that there are two broad approaches within the field of leadership scholarship (see for example Uhl-Bien, 2006). The first of these is described as the *entity* approach – the traditional view of seeing leadership as something a leader does. The focus here is solely on the formal leader and their attributes. I describe the second approach as the *entity-relational* approach, which focuses on how leaders interact with their followers and includes established theories such as transformational / transactional leadership as well as newer research around empowering, and ethical and servant leadership.

There is then a wealth of criticism around leadership studies, particularly around this 'blind faith' in the leadership phenomenon and centred on the failure of researchers to provide clear definitions and remove ambiguity, which has led to weak theoretical development (e.g. Alvesson & Blom, 2015; Alvesson & Spicer, 2012; Blom & Alvesson, 2015; Calder, 1977). Nonetheless, whilst it is undoubtedly difficult to nail down clear meanings of concepts such as leadership, management and organisational behaviours, it is surely important to continue to push forward with research that attempts to remove ambiguity and contribute to a clear overall picture of what may, or may not be happening in organisations. Even some of the most vocal critics of approaches to leadership studies agree that it has a potentially valuable element in making organisations function (Alvesson & Spicer, 2012).

Does leadership matter in planned events and event tourism?

Event studies grew out of an interest in the impact of event tourism from tourism academics, led by Professor Donald Getz. Since his seminal works into event studies in the early 2000s, interest in event management has grown and event studies have become a distinct discipline. In the early days, academic literature largely reflected this interest in tourism in relation to events – they therefore focussed on areas such as the economic impacts of events and the motivations and perceptions of visitors, attendees or residents (Getz, 2000; Harris, Jago, Allen, & Huyskens, 2001; Mair & Whitford, 2013; Wood, Robinson, & Thomas, 2004). Since the early 2010s however, there has been an expansion of research approaches (Bladen, Kennell, Abson, & Wilde, 2012; Dredge & Whitford, 2010; Mair & Whitford, 2013) which has included a move towards event research that focuses on issues such as the environmental impact of events, positive and negative event impacts, technical aspects of operations and management, social capital and political involvement (e.g. Ali-Knight & Robertson, 2004; Arcodia & Whitford, 2007; Dwyer, Jago, & Forsyth, 2015; Fairley, 2016; Filo, 2016; Finkel, McGillivray, McPherson, & Robinson, 2013; Mair & Jago, 2010). There is also a small, but growing body of research that explores the negative impacts of event management and the *"overwhelmingly uncritical and self-congratulatory"* nature of the events industry (Rojek, 2014, p. 32). However, whilst research into events is evolving and expanding quickly, the majority of published research still concentrates largely on either the tangible aspects of the event delivery, such as motivating volunteers, stakeholder management and the use of technology in event management; or on the outcomes of the event itself, such as customer satisfaction, return on investment, and short- or long-term legacies (Mair & Whitford, 2013; Park & Park, 2017; Pernecky, 2015), and little empirical research has been conducted that focuses on aspects of organisational behaviour or the human resource.

There are still, then, areas of focus which scholars have yet to turn to – a pressing example of this is that there is very little empirical research that focuses specifically on the working processes of event organisations, and in particular, the nature and dynamics of leadership within this context (Megheirkouni, 2018). An analysis of published literature by Park and Park (2017) found that only 4.2% of research papers published in event management journals focussed on aspects of HR. Whilst there is an implicit agreement in much of the leading literature that there are a set of soft management and leadership skills that are essential to the role, yet very little research has been conducted into organisational management, human resource aspects and, in particular, leadership that occurs in experiential event organisations. This is a problematic gap in our knowledge and understanding of this economic and socially important sector, especially given that events are a service led industry, in which the human resource is the central element for success. As I pointed out in an earlier piece of research into leadership in events:

> *"Event managers believe that it is not the technical skills (such as financial planning, event design) that ensure successful event delivery but rather that it is the soft skills and the human resource that drive successful events .... to be successful leaders, they also need to work in teams, motivate and empower others, and develop team members."*
> (Abson, 2017).

The event / event tourism industry is an interesting setting through which to consider leadership because of several managerial and organisational challenges that are viewed as being unique to this sector. These challenges arise from working within industries that are fast paced, diverse, highly competitive and change rapidly. In addition, the sector has a number of unique characteristics – summarised as the time-bound and peripatetic nature of events (short in duration and often one-off or rotating around a number of locations); diverse in scale and emphasis; highly dependent on a range of teams and organisations to deliver the events and often on volunteers to run the events. In order to run successful planned event and event tourism experiences in this changing and challenging environment, organisations need employees with a wide range of expertise, and skills that include technical, emotional, aesthetic, problem-solving and information-processing (Baum et al., 2009; Bladen et al., 2012; Brown, 2014; Muskat & Mair, 2020; Rutherford Silvers et al., 2006).

Planned events are therefore a particularly interesting lens through which to further enhance our knowledge of leadership because they operate within these urgent, creative, complex working conditions. The very nature of planning and delivering experiences adds a range of different considerations that other industries do not face and those working in the event industry therefore require a certain way of working, that includes the need to be agile, to collaborate with a wide range of people and to share working practices across a range of teams, external and internal (Muskat & Mair, 2020). Figure 1.1 gives us an understanding of what effective event leaders do.

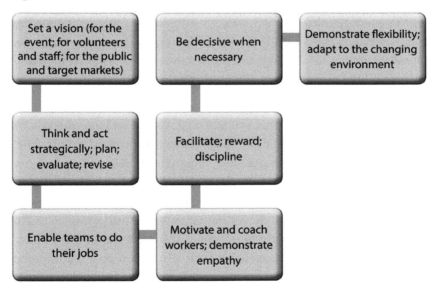

Figure 1.1: What do event managers do? Getz & Page, 2020 (adapted from Abson, 2017)

Leadership in events requires the creation of a vision and a set of goals, the development of the strategy to meet those goals and the ability to inspire a wide variety of stakeholders to work together to achieve them(Getz & Page, 2020). It is this complexity that makes the management of event experience an interesting context for exploring leadership.

Leadership in the event literature

The problem with research into leadership in events is threefold – first, there is a limited quantity, and that which exists is lacking in variety; second, it fails to sufficiently consider how interactions with co-workers, subordinates, others within the organisation and the wider network effects leadership processes (Yukl, 1999); and third, there is not enough empirically informed work. We therefore know relatively little about who leads within event organisations and about how the specific context of planning events impacts on the leadership process.

Whilst there is very little empirical research that focuses specifically on the nature and dynamics of leadership within planned events and event tourism, there is an implicit agreement within much of the leading literature that leadership is essential to the role. In order to give the reader a clear understanding of the current thinking of leadership within event literature, it is useful to summarise some of the leading events scholars' views on the subject. As such, below is an annotated literature review of the key textbooks coverage of leadership within events and the event management industry.

Getz & Page (2020)

In the fourth series of this seminal text, Getz and Page discuss the importance of leadership in the management of planned events. They draw attention to the management functions of event planning, and focus briefly on leadership (see page 344). The text gives a brief summary of the six schools of leadership theory identified by Dulewicz and Higgs (2003) and then delves into a variety of leadership roles and styles, offering useful insight into a range of current thinking on leadership. What is particularly useful is their discussion on organisational culture and leadership, and the dynamics of planned events that make event leadership complex.

Van der Wagen (2006)

Van der Wagen outlines the need to understand and develop human capital effectively and explains why leadership matters in events, discussing how events managers are leading projects that are *"creative, complex, problematic, dynamic or stakeholder reliant"* (p. 216) and that in order to do this successfully, they must possess vision and leadership. Van der Wagen suggests these skills should be based around the ability to transform situations, to hold a creative vision and, crucially, must include strong decision-making skills. Her text has a chapter on leadership which implies that leadership is an integral part of event management – describing the context of leadership in events and the relevance of leadership theories, but stops short of indicating which school of leadership is most relevant to event management, or which leadership skills and styles are required for the day to day management of event projects. This work is now over 10 years old and therefore the theoretical foundations she draws on are out-dated; yet her text is included here because it is still relied upon by teaching academics as a seminal piece of work on HR in events.

Bladen, Kennell, Abson and Wilde (2018)

Bladen et al., move beyond the acknowledgement that event managers do lead, which is implicit within Van der Wagen's text, and instead make the clear link between the type of leadership, the culture of the team and the style of the event delivery. Importantly, the discussion in this text centres on the shift from a concentration on the tools and techniques of project management leadership to a focus on the need for leadership competencies in order to deliver successful events. The suggestion here is that, in the early studies of event management, leading authors in the field concentrated on goal-orientated leadership. However, Bladen et al. argue that this leadership style is not workable in the events industry, as the industry does not operate within stable environments. Instead, events are described as transitory – core project variables such as plans and resources are often in a state of flux and the projects are fluid and event managers therefore need to be involving and engaging leaders in order to deliver successful projects. Whilst interesting, this textbook is not empirically grounded and does not draw on primary research from any of the inter-related disciplines in order to inform or support the perception of leadership within events. The text also has a tendency towards a view of leadership only as a set of skills or competencies – this viewpoint will be explored in Chapter 6 of this book.

Goldblatt (2008 / 2014)

Professor Goldblatt publishes a very well-respected textbook which is now on its 7th edition. Goldblatt refers to event leadership throughout this book, but does so with a more holistic view of the term 'leadership' – his book focuses on all event management as the leading of events. For him, the profession of event management has evolved from managing resources and securing logistics to the need to have a body of knowledge that incorporates strategic planning but also includes leadership skills that *are needed for long-term career success*" (Goldblatt, 2008, p. xiv). Goldblatt offers three leadership styles relevant to the industry – laissez-faire, autocratic and democratic, and gives a brief description of each. These are the same styles of leadership that are discussed in Bladen et al., but there is much debate around the ambiguity of leadership being able to be pared back to a discussion of stylistic behaviour. Whilst there is a strong focus on leadership styles, leadership theory is not discovered in sufficient detail for the reader to understand the scale and diversity of it and how it impacts on event management.

Bowdin, Allen, O'Toole, Harris and McDonnell (2011)

The Bowdin et al. text is similar in content and readership to the Bladen et al. text. It is similar too, in that it focuses on how to manage the human resource at events, but does not give specific space to the consideration of leadership theory other than to include a view of leadership as a set of skills or competencies. So, whilst useful as an indicator of the importance of leadership in planned events, the focus is somewhat limited in scope.

Baum, Deery, Hanlon, Lockstone, and Smith (eds) (2009

This edited book gives a comprehensive review of the range of work that exists within the event industry. In doing so, it touches occasionally on leadership but never in any detail. That this excellent collection of work about employment in events does not cover leadership in any great detail is perhaps the biggest indication of the way leadership has thus far been neglected in the event literature.

The workforce of the future and events careers

Recent macro and micro influences in business, such as changes to economic forecasts, political unrest and improved technology – and of course, the global pandemic of Covid-19, have resulted in emerging challenges to leadership in organisations. Organisations are now being asked to be adaptive, creative and innovative, and employees are expected to work collaboratively, across a range of functions, with people from around the globe. With the digitalisation of the workplace, the growing ubiquity of mobile technologies and a culture of connectivity, a different set of leadership capabilities are now required. Leadership therefore takes place in a constantly changing and challenging environment, with a shifting workforce demographic which currently sees five generations working together at once.

In particular, the management of events currently faces some serious managerial and organisational challenges. These can be viewed as global challenges – such as those brought about by the Covid-19 virus outbreak in 2020 or the terrorist acts in event spaces, such as the Manchester Arena bombing in 2017 – and those that are viewed as being unique to the events industry. These challenges can be summarised as working within an industry that was brought almost to a complete halt by Covid-19, but also one that is traditionally fast paced, diverse, highly competitive and changeable. In order to run successful events in this changing and challenging environment, event managers need a wide range of technical and soft skills. In particular, as they manage events in a time when the economy is hard hit, leisure spending is down, and the recession has resulted in loss of marketing spend, leadership has never been more important. Finding ways to deliver experiences that matter in these circumstances, and ensuring that those experiences offer positive social and community leadership, as well as the more usual objectives of profit or networking, requires leadership on a scale never seen before. And the intricacies of leading complex experiences still remain – managing teams that 'pulsate' throughout the event delivery period, and which are always interconnected and heavily reliant on each other to deliver a successful event, but rarely in the same room, building or even organisations, alongside the ever-increasing emphasis on technological usage and a requirement for an international outlook. This book therefore seeks to provide insight for those working in, and those studying, event organisations. Event managers, and event organisations, must become more agile in their working practices in order to keep pace with the changing environment that they are operating within.

Leadership in action: Industry insight from Lils Collingwood, Albany Appointments

Lils Collingwood, company owner and director, took over Albany in 2019 after joining the business in 2017. She studied Events Management at University of Greenwich and worked for Wembley Stadium for 3 years before moving into the commercial world of business conferences, exhibitions and events. As well as running Albany Appointments, Lils co-hosts The Agenda, a monthly panel show with five female event professionals. Every month they invite special guests and discuss hot topics in the events industry.

What employers want from event graduates

Albany has been recruiting for the media, conference and events industry for over 30 years. When it comes to reading CVs and managing client expectations, we have seen it all: the good, the bad and the ugly!

Working in events is incredibly competitive, and I often warn candidates the two hardest stages of their career are getting their foot in the door, and reaching the top. Once you're in, you're in – but persuading a hiring manager to give you that first chance is one of the biggest hurdles every graduate will face.

When recruiting for entry level events roles, there are a few triggers that make me pick up the phone to invite someone to an interview. One of the most important things we look for in a CV is "get-go". By "get-go" I mean a person who is passionate, committed and captivating.

A CV where there is little beyond desk-based learning simply isn't enough for a hiring manager. That may even suggest the candidate chose the subject merely due to lack of direction and inspiration, not because it is genuinely a career goal.

So how can you show "get-go" on a two-page document? Well, beyond showing commitment to university and consistency with grades, it's about going out of your way to make opportunities happen: volunteering, taking an industry placement year, and throwing yourself at every chance to build up hands-on, real-world experience. Learning about events through books is a world away from learning by being onsite at live events. As an event management student, it is your job to bridge the gap between the two.

There are some simple things students can do so the world of real live events isn't so alien to them. First, keep your ear to the ground. Read industry magazines, follow thought leaders and engage with industry peers on LinkedIn. Don't be afraid to network, get talking to people who work in events. Ask questions and listen to others. Engage in conversations: both in person and online.

Attend events, see them first-hand, and above all *feel them*. Events are an immersive experience, which can only be truly understood when you are there. Observe it from both an attendee and production perspective. Everything you see: the layout of the room, the content and agenda, the choice of speakers, the sponsorship branding, visual design of the programme; all of these elements have been carefully curated by different teams who put the show together. It's worth making a mental note of which of these individual elements spark your interest. These early observations can lay the foundations of your career plan and help you decide which area you'd like to specialise in. This can be used as the starting point to building experience within these niches.

Then be brave and put your own content out there, share your observations. It is perfectly fine to convey your thoughts as someone new to the industry. Start a dialogue where you invite those with more experience to join the discussion and share their insight. Not only will this raise your credibility as a budding events professional, it will improve your personal brand and shape how others (potential hiring managers) see you. Personal branding is everything when it comes to your career. Don't see LinkedIn as an online CV, but as a place to get noticed by those you'd like to work for.

What matters is that you are making those steps to be a front-runner against your university peers and demonstrating yourself as an independent thinker. You want to be seen as someone who has taken the time to understand a niche, who's observed events first-hand, and is unafraid to share with others and start a dialogue. Post content, whether that is a blog, videos, or podcast series, sharing your observations or asking questions on key topics. Be creative! I can guarantee, it's that kind of *get-go* that will make you a head above the rest.

When it comes to applying for events roles, use your CV and cover letter to showcase your attitude and get-go, and provide examples of where you've thrown yourself into learning about the industry you've chosen to be part of. A CV should outline the facts, whereas a cover letter should tell a story. If you can nail the two, don't be surprised if you start receiving calls from recruiters and hiring managers!

About Albany Appointments

Albany Appointments is an established recruitment agency for the B2B conference, events and media industry. They have recruited for events, media and publishing for over 30 years, their strength lies in their comprehensive knowledge and experience within the industry, as well as the service commitment to clients and candidates.

Study questions

Each of the learning objectives suggests one or more study or discussion questions, as the reader should be able to demonstrate the applicable knowledge drawn from this and subsequent chapters. Further questions that could be integrated into study might be:

1 Discuss the nature of professionalism within events and event tourism, with reference to leadership. Describe the knowledge and skills needed to be an event manager, and discuss how leadership fits within this.

2 Describe why leadership matters in planned events and event tourism. What makes these settings unique and how might that change the types of leadership required?

3 Discuss the difference between leadership and management.

4 How would you define leadership?

5 Develop your own definition of 'good' leadership. What does leadership mean to you?

6 Develop your own definition of 'bad' leadership. To help, think of the worst boss you have ever had – why do you think they were such bad leaders?

Further reading

Bladen, C. Kennell, J., Abson, E. & Wilde, N. (2018) *Event Management: An introduction.* London: Routledge.

EMBOK: Event Management Body of Knowledge (https://www.embok.org/index.php/embok-model).

Getz, D. & Page, S. (2020) *Event Studies* (4th edition) London: Routledge.

Kotterman, J. (2006) Leadership versus Management: What's the difference. *Journal for Quality and Participation.* **29**(2), 13-17.

MBECS: Meetings & Business Events Competency Standards (https://mpi.org).

References

Abson, E. (2017) How event manager's lead – applying competency school theory to event management. *Event Management,* **21**(4), 403-419.

Ali-Knight, J., & Robertson, M. (2004). Introduction to arts, culture and Leisure in festival and event management: an international arts and culture perspective. In I. Yeoman, M. Robertson, J. Ali-Knight, U. McMachon-Beattie, & S. Drummond (Eds.), *Festivals and Events Management: an international arts and culture perspective* (pp. 3-13). Oxon: Butterworth-Heinemann.

Alvesson, M. & Blom, M. (2015). Less followership, less leadership? An inquiry into the basic but seemingly forgotten downsides of leadership. *Management,* **18**(3), 266-282.

Alvesson, M. & Spicer, A. (2012). Critical leadership studies: the case for critical performativity. *Human Relations,* **65**(3), 367-390. doi:10.1177/0018726711430555.

Arcodia, C. & Whitford, M. (2007). Festival attendance and the development of social capital. *Journal of Convention & Event Tourism,* **8**(2), 1-18. doi:10.1300/J452v08n02_01.

Avolio, B. J., Walumbwa, F. O. & Weber, T. J. (2009). Leadership: current theories, research and future directions. *Annual Review of Psychology,* **60**, 421-429.

Badaracco, J. (2001). We don't need another hero. *Harvard Business Review,* **79**(8), 120-126.

Banks, G. C., Gooty, J., Ross, R. L., Williams, C. E. & Harrington, N. T. (2018). Construct redundancy in leader behaviours: a review and agenda for the future. *Leadership Quarterly,* **29**(1), 236-251.

Baum, T., Deery, M., Hanlon,. C., Lockstone, L. & Smith, K. (eds) (2009*). People and Work in Events and Conventions: a research perspective.* Oxford: CABI.

Bladen, C., Kennell, J., Abson, E. & Wilde, N. (2012). *Events Management : An introduction.* London: Routledge.

Blom, M. & Alvesson, M. (2015). All-inclusive and all good: the hegemonic ambiguity of leadership. *Scandinavian Journal of Management,* **31**(4), 480-92.

Brown, S. (2014). Emerging professionalism in the event industry: A practitioner's perspective. *Event Management,* **18**, 15-24. doi:10.3727/1525 99514X13883555341760.

Calder, B. (1977). An attribution theory of leadership. In B. M. Staw & G. R. Salanick (Eds.), *New Directions in Organisational Behaviour.* Chicago: St Clair.

Dredge, D. & Whitford, M. (2010). Policy for sustainable and responsible festivals and events: institutionalisation of a new paradigm – a response. *Journal of Policy Research in Tourism, Leisure and Events,* **2**(1), 1-13. doi:10.1080/19407960903542235.

Dulewicz, V. & Higgs, M. (2003) *Design of a new instrument to assess leadership dimensions and styles.* Henley Working paper 0311. Henley Management College. Available at: www.henleymc.ac.uk

Dwyer, L., Jago, L. & Forsyth, P. (2015). Economic evaluation of special events: Reconciling economic impact and cost–benefit analysis. *Scandinavian Journal of Hospitality and Tourism,* **16**(2), 115-129. doi:10.108 0/15022250.2015.1116404.

Fairley, S. (2016). The spirit lives on: The legacy of volunteering at the Sydney 2000 Olympic Games. *Event Management,* **20**(2), 201-215.

Filo, K. (2016). Exploring the positive psychology domains of well-being activated through charity sport event experiences. *Event Management,* **20**(2), 181-199. doi:10.3727/152599516X14610017108701.

Finkel, R., McGillivray, D., McPherson, G. & Robinson, P. (Eds.). (2013). *Research Themes for Events.* Oxon: CABI.

Getz, D. (2000, July). *Developing a research agenda for the event management field.* Paper presented at the Events Beyond 2000, Sydney.

Getz, D. & Page, S., (2020). *Event Studies : Theory, Research and Policy for Planned Events* (4th Ed). Abingdon: Routledge.

Goldblatt, J. (2008). *Special Events: Event Leadership for a New World* (5th ed.). New Jersey: John Wiley & Sons.

Harris, R., Jago, L., Allen, J. & Huyskens, M. (2001). Towards an Australian event research agenda *Event Management,* **6**(4), 213-221.

Kotterman, J. (2006) Leadership versus Management: What's the difference. *Journal for Quality and Participation.* **29**(2), 13-17.

Mair, J. & Jago, L. (2010). The development of a conceptual model of greening in the business events tourism sector. *Journal of Sustainable Tourism,* **18**(1), 77-94. doi:10.1080/09669580903291007.

Mair, J. & Whitford, M. (2013). An exploration of events research: event topics, themes and emerging trends. *International Journal of Event and Festival Management,* **4**(1), 6-30. doi:10.1108/17582951311307485.

Megheirkouni, M. (2018). Insights on practicing of servant leadership in the events sector. *Sport, Business and Management,* **8**(2), 134-152.

Muskat, B. & Mair, J. (2020). Knowledge sharing and power in the event workforce. *Event Management, Pre-publication.*

Park, S. B. & Park, K. (2017). Thematic trends in event management research. *International Journal of Contemporary Hospitality Management,* **29**(3), 848-861.

Pernecky, T. (2015). Sustainable leadership in event management. *Event Management,* **19**(1), 109-121. doi:10.3727/152599515X14229071393188

Rojek, C. (2014). Global Event Management: a critique. *Leisure Studies,* **33**(1), 32-47.

Rutherford Silvers, J., Bowdin, G. A. J., O'Toole, W., J. & Beard Nelson, K. (2006). Towards an International Event Management Body of Knowledge (EMBOK). *Event Management,* **9**(4), 185-198.

Uhl-Bien, M. (2006). Relational leadership theory: exploring the social processes of leadership and organizing. *Leadership Quarterly,* **17**(6), 654-676.

Van der Wagen, L., (2006) *Human Resource Management for Events.* London: Routledge

Wood, E. H., Robinson, L. & Thomas, R. (2004). *The contribution of community festivals on tourism: an assessment of the impacts of rural events in Wales*. Paper presented at the Assessing the impact of tourist events, University Nice.

Yammarino, F. J. (2013). Leadership: Past, present and future. *Journal of Leadership & Organisational Studies, 20*(2), 149-155.

Yukl, G. (2010). *Leadership in Organisations* (3rd ed.). New Jersey: Pearson.

2 Classic approaches to leadership

Chapter aims

- ☐ Introduce and critically discuss the classic theories of leadership
- ☐ Understand the meaning of 'entity' leadership
- ☐ Critically examine leadership behavioural theory
- ☐ Explore the concept of leading through contingencies
- ☐ Compare the strengths and weaknesses of the classic theories of leadership
- ☐ Focus on leadership in action: being an event entrepreneur by Jason Scott Allan.

Classic approaches to leadership – entity approaches

This chapter summarises the classic theories of leadership. The reader will note the similarities that exist within this area of leadership studies – these theories all focus on the individual leader, and view leadership as a specialised role. In these classic approaches to leadership, leadership is something someone 'does', and the focus is solely on the formal leader and their personality characteristics or their attributes. These approaches are now sometimes referred to as entity leadership because leadership is the sole preserve of the entity or individual, and that individual is highly influential. These theories of leadership began to emerge in the late nineteenth and early twentieth century, and whilst they are now between 50 and 100 years old, it is important to explore them briefly, as they form the basis from which leadership studies first emerged.

At this stage, I remind the reader of the key point I made in the introductory chapter to this book – whilst the field of leadership is perhaps one of the most studied subjects in history, event management academics have yet to fully turn their attention to it. That is why, when you read through the next few chapters on specific leadership theory, you won't see a lot of references to specific event research.

Trait or Great Man leadership – what are leaders like?

One of the oldest ways of thinking about leadership is through trait theories or the trait approach – sometimes known as 'The Great Man Theory.' Trait theories emerged sometime during the end of the nineteenth and the start of the twentieth century, and revolved around the notion that certain personality characteristics make someone a leader. The trait approach suggests that people are born to be leaders – that there is a generic set of traits that leaders are born with – a set of extraordinary abilities – such as foresight, persuasive powers and intuition (Bass, 1990; Cawthon, 1996). Jago, writing in the 1980s, summarised the traits thought to signify leadership as physical (e.g. height, weight, hair, clothes); personality (e.g. aggression, dominance, enthusiasm, sense of humour); social (e.g. prestige, tact); skill (e.g. intelligence, judgement, knowledge) [List adapted from Jago, by Taylor, 2019].

Looking back on these first attempts to understand leadership, it is easy to be critical. Questions should immediately arise, such as – how did these 'leaders' get to be in the position of power in the first place? And which of the 100s of personality traits that exist really matter? And why are leaders always men…

The core issue is therefore the simplistic nature of trait theory. Simply identifying the presence of traits does not explain why those people are leading, or how those traits are contributing to leadership. And nor does it allow us to examine good or bad leadership – how do we know that the presence of a physical trait such as height results in effective leadership? Well of course we don't, because the presence of a physical trait alone is not enough for us to predict leadership effectiveness.

Importantly, it is also impossible for us to imagine that one person can possess all the leadership traits needed to run an event, all at the same time. Can you think of one event leader who was always positive, enthusiastic, aggressive, dominant, intelligent, funny and empathetic all at once, no matter what the situation is?! The key criticism of trait theory then is that it is far too narrow and far too static – leadership cannot be boiled down to the possession of number of personality or physical traits, and cannot discount other important factors such as the way people behave, the context within which leadership occurs or the people who accept leadership (the followers).

The assumption within these trait theories was that if these personal characteristics or traits of a leader could be identified, the concept of leadership can be understood. However, as the seminal work by Stodgill, in 1948 showed, the studies conducted in the 1930s and 1940s failed to find any traits that would result in leadership success. Stodgill carried out a literature review of the first four decades of the 20th Century, attempting to identify and summarise the common themes and personality traits associated with leadership. This review demonstrated that whilst traits are an important part of the leadership picture, the results of the hundreds of studies Stodgill reviewed were inconclusive. In fact, a large number of traits emerged in different studies which were seen as descriptive of leaders but none of the research provided statistically significant differences in traits between the average person and a leader. Stodgill, then, concluded that people do not become leaders by virtue of the traits they possess, but that significant numbers of traits are important for people in leadership positions.

It is important to note that trait theory, whilst often dismissed in leadership literature, still has value today. Whilst scholars have rejected the genetic nature of trait theory (people are not born to be leaders) and have largely dismissed the traits such as sex, height and weight as being essential descriptors for 'good' leadership, there is still plenty of research that focuses on personality traits as important contributors to leadership. Northouse (2015), for example, reviews some of the major research findings within trait theory and concludes that there are six specific traits that people need to be leaders. These are intelligence, confidence, charisma, determination, sociability and integrity. And in a review of research into trait theory, Xu and colleagues (2014) demonstrate that there is now a contemporary view of trait theory, which includes a wider range of traits and looks at things like how traits might evolve over time, and under different situations. These contemporary views of trait theory tend to see traits as changeable, which is where they differ from the classic 'great man' view, in which traits are seen as unchanging parts of a person's personality.

So, identifying which personality traits are helpful for effective leadership is still a prominent part of leadership studies, and still a significant part of the recruitment process for planned events (for example, think about psychometric testing – what are they really, if not a test for inherent personality traits?) Think for example of an event entrepreneur like Michael Eavis, who founded Glastonbury Festival. Do you think he was born to be entrepreneurial? Do you think his personality traits have been integral to the creation of Glastonbury Festival, to seek out all the opportunities needed to run it every year and to take the personal and financial risks it involved in the early years? Do you believe he has the personality traits needed to lead the festival? If so, then you are applying the trait theory of leadership.

Back in 1948, Stodgill's work is largely agreed to have closed off the research that centred on the idea that men were born to be great leaders. We'll return to Stodgill's study later in this chapter, when we explore further how his seminal work changed leadership studies.

Behavioural theories of leadership – what do leaders do?

Stodgill's work provoked a paradigm shift in the study of leadership. At first, debates raged around individualism and the value attached to one 'heroic' leader, with the core disagreement stemming from just how much influence one person can have. As the criticisms grew, scholars sought to find alternative explanations of what makes people good leaders, and how to distinguish between leaders and non-leaders. This led to researchers looking towards specific skills and attributes that leaders should have, and the way they behave – hence the emergence of the behavioural studies, which focused on the behaviours associated with effective leadership (Kirkpatrick & Locke, 1991; Yukl, 2010). For some, this meant that, if it isn't who people are that provides a universally insight into leadership, perhaps it is what they do. Researchers began to investigate how leaders behaved (Bass, 1990; Bass & Bass, 2008). The starting point for the theories that emerged from this approach can be seen as acknowledging that just possessing the right combination of traits does not make a person a leader; it simply makes it more likely that people possessing these traits will take the right actions to be successful.

Kirkpatrick and Locke (1991) attempted to bridge the gap between the trait approach and newer behavioural theories – they proposed that traits do matter and that there is a set of traits that provide an individual with the right skills to be an effective leader.

"Key leader traits include: drive (a broad term which includes achievement, motivation, ambition, energy, tenacity, and imitative); leadership motivation (the desire to lead but not to seek power as an end in itself); honesty and integrity; self-confidence (which is associated with emotional stability); cognitive ability; and knowledge of the business. There is less clear evidence for traits such as charisma, creativity and flexibility." (Kirkpatrick & Locke, 1991, p. 48).

Having these traits, however, is not enough – leaders must take actions to be successful, and these actions can include setting goals, role modelling or formulating a vision. A key point made by Kirkpatrick and Locke was that *"Leaders are not like other people"* (1991: 59) – whilst leaders might not have to be Great Men, they need to have the *'right stuff'* to succeed (Cawthon, 1996).

These early views of behavioural leadership were looking at the kind of behaviours that leadership exhibited – behavioural leadership theory suggests that people have access to a range of possible ways of behaving and that they have a preference for the kind of behaviour that feels natural to them. They represented a more balanced approach than the trait theories – a less 'heroic' way of doing leadership, which concentrated more on the actions that people took rather than the natural born ability. However, there are clearly limitations to this early school of thought regarding behavioural approach – the first of these is that early scholars considered leadership actions and behaviours to be innate; leaders behaved in certain ways instinctively. The key problem with this school of thought is that it is impossible for one person to innately possess all the leadership behaviours that are required. This is the same argument as the problems with leadership traits – can you think of one leader that possess all the excellent personality traits needed to lead an event, and instinctively knows what actions to take and when? I am willing to bet that you cannot – instead, you might be able to identify some people who exhibit some of the more prominent personality traits needed (such as creativity, enthusiasm or decisiveness) and whom then surround themselves with a team which 'plugs the gaps' for them. Together, they might possess all the leadership behaviours and personality traits which are impossible to find in one person.

It should be noted that the way in which leaders behave is still very much part of leadership studies – theory has, however, evolved into the more specific topic of leadership styles. These later theories differentiate from the early schools of behavioural study because they extend to the consideration of followers as well and they acknowledge that leadership actions, behaviours and styles can be learnt. These theories are explored in detail in Chapter 3.

Is there a place for trait and behavioural theory in the contemporary study of events?

The questions for those of us studying planned events is whether these approaches to understanding leadership via the lens of personality traits or behaviours still hold any value. For instance, does understanding the specific personality traits of an event manager help us to shed light on how to deliver effective experiences? As we saw in Chapter 1, lots of contemporary discussions around leadership in events do still focus on the type of person you need to be to run events. We hear, often, that event managers need to be visionary, creative, influential and decisive, for example. And event managers continue to be assessed on their psychological personality traits through psychometric testing. This then indicates that some of the foundations of trait theory are still useful in trying to understand what makes a good event leader – personality does have some part to play in influencing who becomes a leader and who does not. But can knowing which personality traits and behaviours exist in our leaders give us the full picture? Consider this scenario:

The event manager of a local council is in charge of a local community festival, and needs to manage a range of stakeholders, leading them all to the successful delivery of the event. The list of stakeholders might look something like this:

2: Classic approaches to leadership

Internal stakeholders

- Your event team at the council
- Sponsors of the event
- The council leadership team
- The council marketing team
- The stall holders at the event
- Supplier networks
- Council staff responsible for licensing / road closures etc.

External stakeholders

- The attendees from the local community (who can be further divided, depending on their specific wants, needs and motivations)
- Police & transport networks
- The local community (who can be divided multiple times, depending on their interest in your event)
- Local news agencies (including papers, social media etc)
- Local businesses
- Local transport hubs.

Each of these stakeholders will demand a different level of input from the event leader. Some – such as the staff in your team and your suppliers – will need direction and management. Others – such as the local media agencies, or local transport hubs – will just need you to keep them informed. All of them will have different interests and require different outcomes from the event. Will being the right weight or height help the event manager to lead on this project? Well of course not. But having a high level of enthusiasm might, and so might be empathetic of the various viewpoints and tactful in communicating with the various groups. But just being enthusiastic or tactful is surely not enough to explain whether someone is a good leader or not?

Ultimately, this is the issue with both the behavioural approach and the trait approach – they insist that the individual is the only thing that matters in effective leadership. However, as leadership studies advanced to the mid-twentieth century, scholars realised that viewing a set of traits or behaviours was still not enough to explain effective leadership – and so they began to consider whether the situation within which the leader found themselves was also important.

Contingency leadership – what leaders do depends on the situation

Returning to that key study by Stodgill, back in 1948, which helped researchers to understand that the traits leaders possess cannot be the full story in terms of understanding leadership. His key observation in concluding his study was that, whilst traits have some importance in understanding leadership behaviour, it is the context within which leadership occurred that matters. In other words, people who are leaders in one situation may not be leaders in another. It is the context that matters – the social, cultural or organisational surroundings that the people were working within impacted on the presence – or absence – of leadership traits. It was this observation that led to another shift in leadership studies, in which leadership stopped being characterised solely by individual traits and personality differences, and instead began to also incorporate the situation in which leadership took place.

In 1968, Mischel challenged the prevailing assumption that personality was the most important factor in predicting behaviour and instead argued that situations are at least as important in determining what a person does as their personality. He supported this claim by reviewing previous research to show that the relation between personality and behaviour is not particularly strong. So, according to Mischel, a person who scores high on agreeableness does not necessarily react in an agreeable way in different circumstances. Behaviour began to be considered as a product of both personality and context – and this filtered through to research into leadership. As research into leadership behaviour advanced, and as the science of psychology became more prevalent, it became clear that simply considering personality traits and the way that a person behaves will not provide a clear picture of leadership. Scholars began to realise that the situation or circumstances in which leadership took place had an enormous impact on the way that leaders conducted themselves.

The idea that people will change their leadership styles depending on the situation therefore grew and another shift in leadership research began – this became known as the contingency school (Dinh et al., 2014; Dionne et al., 2014). The basic premise of these theories is that it is not just who the leader is, or if they engage in the correct behaviours that matters – what is important is that leaders exhibit the right behaviours at the right time. The best course of action is therefore contingent on the situation. These early contingency theories therefore focused on the different leadership traits and behaviours and how they changed in different contexts. The key thrust of this school of thought was a challenge to the trait / behavioural theories – even if the leader is enacting successful leadership in one particular moment in time, when the situation changes, there is no guarantee that the same leadership will work. An example of this in the event industry would be the difference between the leadership needed when pitching an event idea to a new client compared to the leadership needed when a serious accident happens on site. In the first situation, a leader exhibiting traits such as creativity, ambition and enthusiasm would be important. In the second situation, the leader needs to demonstrate a personality that is at once calm, decisive and urgent. Consider also the need for change during the event delivery – a leader might get away with being driven and motivational during the smooth delivery of an event, but if their artist doesn't turn up, their drive and motivation won't resolve the problem.

The contingency approach therefore emphasises the importance of contextual factors such as the nature of the work, the type of organisation and the nature of the external environment (Yukl, 2010). The central question is really quite simple – how is leadership affected by context?

The key work here was the contingency model developed by Fiedler (1978). Fiedler developed a theory of leadership effectiveness which is rooted in an individual's leadership style and the degree to which the situation in which they find themselves in enables their ability to exert influence over a group of followers (Cullen, 2019). Fiedler describes the extent to which a leader can exert influence over a group of followers as the 'favourableness' of the situation. For him the favourableness of the situation was dependent on three basic situational variables:

♦ The quality of the relationships that the leader has with members of their group (the leader-member relations)

♦ The level of ambiguity that exists in the work the group has to do (how clear is the task structure?)

♦ The power and influence the leader has over their subordinates.

According to this model, the leader can analyse the situation and then decide which type of leadership style or behaviour they should adopt. If the leader has good relationships with subordinates, but holds little power over them, and is asking them to complete structured tasks, then a relationship-orientated style of leadership should be adopted. If, on the other hand, the relationships are good, and positions of power and influence are high and the task is unstructured, then a results-oriented style would be more appropriate.

Although this model was one of the first, and most influential, theories of leadership, it has been criticised as being too rigid and, because it assumes leadership is based on personality, it didn't take into account that leaders need to adjust their styles depending on the situation. Later, research in this area did take into account the changing situation (Ayman et al., 1995) but much of the research remains concerned with comparing two situations, with the independent variables being things like managerial processes or the influence process (Sashkin & Sashkin, 2003; Yukl, 2010). That said, Fielder's theory is an important point in leadership studies history, as it did much to move the study of leadership away from the individualistic approach it had previously been preoccupied with.

Other notable contingency theories are briefly summarised below, with thanks to the work of Cullen (2019) which form the basis of these summaries:

♦ The **path-goal theory** suggests that leadership behaviours should be matched with the employee and work environment in order to achieve specific goals. The leader should engage with behaviours that complement the subordinate and the situation, in order to lead subordinates into choosing the best paths to reach the organisational goals. So leadership is really just about helping followers to find their path to a particular goal. As such, the leader will have to engage in a variety of leadership behaviours depending on the nature of the situation. The path-goal theory in leadership draws heavily on Vroom's motivational model and the concept of expectancy. (See Miner, 2005, p. 97 for clear discussions on Vroom's theories.)

♦ Hersey and Blanchard's **situational theory** – a newer contribution to contingency theory, it is based on three basic factors – the amount of task-orientated behaviour a leader demonstrates; the amount of relationship-orientated behaviour a leader provides and the readiness that organisational members exhibit in performing a specific task, function or objective.

Theory X and Y

A chapter on the classic approaches to leadership cannot be complete without a brief discussion of Douglas McGregor's Theory X and Theory Y and the leadership styles that stem from it. Northouse (2015) offers a really accessible review of this which readers might find useful – much of the summary below is adapted from his work.

In 1960, McGregor wrote *The Human Side of Enterprise,* in which he suggested that managers need to understand their own personal assumptions about human nature in order to understand how they manage their employees. He was particularly interested in how managers view the motivations of the workers and their attitudes to work. McGregor proposed two general theories that explained the way managers approach their employees – Theory X and Theory Y.

Theory X is made up of three assumptions and – if a leader believes these things, then they form a personal leadership style. The assumptions are:

1 People dislike work

2 People need to be directed and controlled

3 People want security, not responsibility

If these assumptions form part of your fundamental beliefs then you probably view employees as lazy, uninterested in their jobs and as a group of people who do not value their work. And that means you are probably quite directive and controlling, because you don't trust your staff. So you'll supervise people closely and you'll be quick to praise and to criticise. You may well engage in the path-goal leadership in that you will remind people of their goal – to get paid – or threaten them with punishment. You'll believe that your employees need your leadership – without it, they won't be motivated to work.

Theory Y is also made up of three assumptions, which when taken together, form a personal leadership style. They are:

1 People like work

2 People are self-motivated

3 People accept and seek responsibility

If these assumptions form part of your fundamental beliefs, then you believe that your employees are capable and interested in working. You won't try to control the workforce, though you may still define what the work requirements are. You'll think that your employees naturally want to work, and you will try to help them to find a passion for what they do. You'll know that when an employee is committed to their work, they are more motivated to do their job. And you'll encourage your team to seek and accept responsibility. You'll aim to support your staff, without controlling or directing them.

Scholars who follow this school of thought suggest that we all hold these basic beliefs about human nature and the way people behave in the workplace and these form the basis of our leadership philosophy. Whether you hold the assumptions represented by Theory X or Theory Y will impact on your behaviour as a leader, and will shape your leadership style.

Leadership style is defined as the behaviours of a leader – it focuses on what leaders do and how they act. Your leadership style is driven by your leadership philosophy and these can be categorised into three areas – authoritarian, democratic and laissez-faire. It's important to note that these three styles are not mutually exclusive – good leaders can draw on each of the styles when the situation demands it. But you may be naturally drawn to one style over another, because of those underpinning assumptions of Theory X and Theory Y.

Authoritarian leadership style

This is very similar to Theory X – authoritarian leaders think their employees need direction and that they should be controlled and told what to do. Authoritarian leaders emphasise that they are in charge, they don't see themselves as part of the team – they run the team. They praise and criticise freely and they set goals and structure the work.

Authoritarian leadership sounds very negative – it represents a rather pessimistic view of others and suggests that employees are directionless and unwilling to do a good job. But is there ever a time when it might be useful? Well think for a second about running a large event on site for the first time. You'll have a number of different people you have to manage – from all the different suppliers, to the temporary workers who have come on board to help you deliver the event. Being able to tell people what needs to be done, when it needs to be done by and what standards you expect will be essential to ensure the event is delivered safely and in the manner your stakeholders expect. So, when event managers are working in highly pressurised, time-precious and risky situations, authoritarian leadership is a very useful tool to draw on.

Democratic leadership style

This is closely related to the assumptions found in Theory Y. Leaders with a democratic leadership style will treat employees as being capable and self-motivated. They won't control their team, instead they will work with them in order to get the best out of them. They'll try to treat everyone fairly, and they will help each team member to achieve their own personal goals. They support and guide rather than direct, and they listen rather than tell. They give objective praise and criticism.

Democratic leadership is therefore a positive style – it tends to result in higher team satisfaction and commitment – their employees tend to be happy in their work and more motivated to work harder. These leaders make more 'we' statements than 'I' statements. But it is a time-consuming leadership style – to be democratic means that you have to spend time with your team, getting to know them and encouraging them. It is therefore more appropriate for the planning stages of events rather than during event delivery.

Laissez-faire leadership style

This one isn't like either Theory X or Theory Y. The laissez-faire leader doesn't try to control their employees like Theory X leaders do, and nor do they try to guide their team, as Theory Y leaders do. In fact, what they do is ignore their employees completely – because of this, it is sometimes known as non-leadership. These leaders exert minimal influence – they are very laid back, and believe that they should just sit back and watch what happens. Employees have the freedom to do whatever they want to do, and they won't get any praise or any criticisms for it.

So what happens when this type of leadership is used? The answer is not much – little is accomplished because there is no direction, and no motivation. Employees prefer some direction – being left completely on their own causes confusion and frustration. Eventually productivity goes down, as employees find little meaning in their work.

Can you think of a time in the planning of events where this might be a good leadership style? I can't!

Event research and leadership style

Wahab, Shahibi, Ali, Abu Bakar, and Amrin (2014) presented a paper at the World Conference on Business Economics and Management, and later published a brief summation of their research that examined the influence of leadership style on event success. Their research was based on 112 event crews running events in Malaysia and their results suggested that people orientated, and decision-making orientated leadership has a positive relationship with event success.

In another interesting conceptual piece, Pernecky (2015) attempts to move the discussion of leadership in events beyond the basic discussion of leadership contained in many of the key texts, by offering an analysis of the Rhineland/Honeybee model. He explores the unique nature of the industry and then seeks to map the challenges in the event industry against the leadership elements and Honeybee philosophy in order to see if it is a relevant approach for sustainable leadership practices in events. The Honeybee leadership style is based around the idea of diligent, cooperative and forward-thinking honeybees working together to lead an organisation. Pernecky concludes that, due to the character of the events industry, it is difficult to adopt the Honeybee philosophy as it stands because events businesses are project-orientated, with a beginning, middle and end, and are reliant on volunteers and short-term contractors.

Summary

So now the reader should have a better understanding of some of the classic approaches to understanding leadership. These can be summarised as follows:

◆ People are born to be leaders. They are genetically disposed to lead and are born with the traits required (Trait theories).

◆ It isn't who people are that make them Great Leaders of Men, it's the way their personality makes them behave that makes them a leader (Behavioural theory).

◆ People are born with leadership traits, and the way they behave is important. But – and crucially – good leadership requires naturally born leaders to adapt their leadership style depending on the situation (Contingency theories).

◆ People hold assumptions about other people. These assumptions shape their leadership style – if they believe people are lazy and need direction, they will become authoritarian, but if they think that people are capable and self-motivated, they will be more democratic in their leadership approach (Theory X and Y and leadership styles).

The reliance on psychometric testing in recruiting event managers suggests that the event industry still continues to believe in the existence of personality traits in order to determine leadership potential. Readers are asked to question this emphasis on personality traits though – if we accept that people are born leaders, then we reject the idea that people's personalities change and evolve over time. This means that there is little chance for leadership development.

The second classic approach merges the principles of leadership traits with the actions and behaviours of leaders; it considers what is it that leaders do. But it still views leadership behaviour through the lens of the individual – it is only the behaviour of the leader that matters. That said, leadership behaviours still form a large part of the conversations around leadership that happen today – these are explored further in Chapter 3.

This contingency approach to leadership does recognise that leadership is not solely related to the individual and that other influences should be considered. The issue here, however, is that these theories relate those external influences back to the individual leader, and focus on how he or she reacts to situational variables. They fail to acknowledge any other relationships that many researchers now feel are vital to effective leadership. In reviews of more recent trends in leadership research, Dinh et al. (2014) and Gardner, Lowe, Moss, Mahoney, and Cogliser (2010) both note that interest in these approaches are on the decline, perhaps because they reached maturity and scholars' interests have gone in a new direction. For many scholars, the new direction involves the consideration of leadership as a dyadic process – it involves both the leader and the follower. As Stodgill concluded:

"A person does not become a leader by virtue of the possession of some combination of traits, but the pattern of personal characteristics of the leader must bear some relevant relationship to the characteristics, activities and goals of the followers." (1948, p. 64)

This move from considering leadership as the preserve of the individual to incorporate those that follow as well is explored in the next chapter.

Leadership in action: Industry insight from Jason Allan Scott, entrepreneur and author

Jason Allan Scott is an award-winning entrepreneur, podcaster, and best-selling author. Various media and social media platforms, including Amazon, have called him a top influencer on the web; Double Dutch said he is one of the most influential event professionals in the world, as did Eventbrite. Jason was recognized as a top 100 small business for his Podcast Production and Teaching Platform and invited to Number 10 Downing Street. He has helped ILEA UK, Arsenal FC, Fulham University, Small Business UK, Google, Canvas Planner, TFN, The Marketing Society, BBC, Marvel, Asemblr, EventMB, WB, Interguide and Holmes Place grow through events, sales, and online marketing. His online marketing has generated several million visitors (38% of them spend money on paid ads), Jason's YouTube videos have had over 1 million views, his podcasts generate over 100,000 listens per month and his podcast school has had a 98% success rate since starting. Jason has spoken at over 210 conferences, events, and companies around the world. From speaking at Google, Oxford, and Coutts to major growth marketing conferences, he now focuses on teaching people to use podcasting for their business and brand and started the world's first exclusive travel deal site for the Meeting Incentive Conferences and Events Newsletter and website www.miceoffers.com.

What leadership means in the event industry, as seen by an entrepreneur

What do the world's most successful entrepreneurs, greatest event managers, and most inspirational business leaders have in common?

They all have a particular mindset, an unwavering focus on progress, and a bold and pioneering outlook. Many are calling this, 'entrepreneurial leadership'. To understand this concept we need to start by understanding leadership. Leadership is the act of guiding a team or individual to achieve a certain goal through direction and motivation; this is nowhere more important than in events where everyone must work together to achieve the goal of the client.

Leadership is defined as *"a process by which a person influences others to accomplish an objective and directs the organization in a way that makes it more coherent and cohesive."* A good leader is one who is always three steps ahead of the others. They look out for the people before others.

John C. Maxwell said, *"a good leader is one who takes a little more than his share of the blame and a little less than his share of the credit."* Leaders are kind, motivating, knowledgeable, and always concerned for the other person. They build excellence and accomplish this by first building character. Understandably, they need to be trusted and prove themselves trustworthy so that people will look up to and admire them. One who strives to be a good leader has to be honest, inspiring, intelligent, and stand firm for what he believes, not backing down.

Entrepreneurs by nature are a special breed. We see the world through entirely different lenses. I've been asked about 'the Entrepreneurial Mind' for years now and how all successful entrepreneurs think in terms of ideas, barriers, and outcomes. You cannot use traditional people-management techniques to get results, as entrepreneurs— we think and behave differently. Instead, entrepreneurs lead with support and guide their team along the way, taking the full weight and responsibility of the success or failure of the project with them.

Leadership through the eyes of an entrepreneur is not about managing people, but rather influencing them through inspiration and motivation to help them achieve outcomes. Leadership, like any other element in our CEO toolkit, requires a strong investment of time and energy; but learning good leadership techniques provides a massive return on investment in the long run.

Although there are many styles of leadership around, my personal leadership philosophy is a simple one that has helped me achieve everything throughout my career: Dream, Build, Inspire, Lead. The beautiful thing is that when you analyse the achievements of other successful entrepreneurs and business leaders, you find we all do the same four things in different ways.

Entrepreneurial leadership involves organizing and motivating a group of people to achieve a common objective through innovation, risk optimization, taking advantage of opportunities, and managing the dynamic organizational environment. The traditional corporate mindset has its focus on systems and processes to mitigate risks, whereas the entrepreneurial mindset is more geared towards taking risks and discovering what works.

Managers need to have both leadership and entrepreneurship qualities in order to be successful. Having one without the other is not enough for success. At this point, the concept of entrepreneurial leadership emerges. Entrepreneurial leadership is a new and modern type of leadership that is a combination of leadership qualities and spirit of entrepreneurship.

The personal characteristics of a successful entrepreneur are self-confidence, determination, communication and persuasion, skills, openness to new ideas, having a vision, using initiative, reliability, positive thinking, flexibility, risk-taking, hard work, organizational ability, the ability to control, knowledge, reconciled with the environment, persistence, rationality, seizing opportunities, and continuous self-renewal.

Sound familiar? These are the qualities of the perfect event planner!

Study questions

1 Do you believe there is such a thing as a natural born leader? If so, what makes them special?

2 What are the main criticisms of the trait approaches to leadership?

3 What personality traits does the contemporary leadership literature suggest an event leader might need? What do you think the list should include?

4 Do you think personalities stay the same throughout people's lives? If not, how does this impact on leadership traits?

5 How useful do you think psychometric testing is in identifying potential leaders? What are the strengths and weaknesses of such tests?

6 Are contingency theories of leadership more suited to crisis situations in event management? Why / why not?

7 Think about McGregor's Theory X and Theory Y. Which set of assumptions most aligns with your own personal beliefs? And what does that mean for your leadership style?

8 In the Leadership in Action section, Jason discusses a number of traits and skills that he believes are important for leaders. Do you agree with his list?

9 In the Leadership in Action section, Jason discusses entrepreneurial leadership. What are the key differences between what he describes and the theories discussed in this chapter?

Further reading

Cawthorn, D. L. (1996). Leadership: the great man theory revisited. (Editorial) *Business Horizons*, **39**, 1.

Cullen, J. (2019). Leading through contingencies. In Carroll, B., Ford, J. & Taylor, S. (eds) *Leadership 2*, pg 68-92, London: Sage.

Jago, A. (1982) Leadership: perspectives in theory and research, *Management Science*, **28** (3), 315-36.

Northouse, P. (2015) *Introduction to Leadership*. London: Sage.

Taylor, S. (2019). Trait theories of leaders and leadership. In Carroll, B., Ford, J. & Taylor, S. (eds) *Leadership 2*, pg 49-67, London: Sage.

References

Ayman, R., Chemers, M. M. & Fiedler, F. (1995). The contingency model of leadership effectiveness: Its levels of analysis. *Leadership Quarterly*, **6**(2), 147-167. doi:10.1016/1048 9843(95)90032-2

Bass, B. M. (1990). *Bass & Stodgill's Handbook of Leadership* (3rd ed.). New York: The Free Press.

Bass, B. M.,& Bass, R. (2008). *The Bass Handbook of Leadership: Theory, research & managerial applications* (4th ed.). New York: Free Press.

Cawthon, D. L. (1996). Leadership: the great man theory revisited (Editorial). *Business Horizons*, **39**(3), 1. doi:10.1016/ S0007-6813(96)90001-4.

Cullen, J. (2019). Leading through contingencies. Carroll, B., Ford, J .& Taylor, S. (eds) *Leadership 2*, pg 68-92, London: Sage.

Dinh, J., Lord, R.G., Gardner, W.L., Meuser, J.D., Liden, R.C. & Hu,J. (2014). Leadership theory and research in the new millennium: Current theoretical trends and changing perspectives. *Leadership Quarterly*, **25**(1), 36-62. doi:http://dx.doi.org/10.1016/j.leaqua.2013.11.005.

Dionne, S., Gupta, A., Sotak, K. L., Shirreffs, K. A., Serban, A., Hao, C., Kim, D. H. & Yammarino, F. J. (2014). A 25-year perspective on levels of analysis in leadership research. *Leadership Quarterly*, **25**(1), 6-35. http://dx.doi.org/10.1016/j.leaqua.2013.11.002.

Fiedler, F. E. (1978). The contingency model and the dynamics of the leadership process. *Advances in Experimental Social Psychology*, **11**, 59-112.

Gardner, W. L., Lowe, K. B., Moss, T. W., Mahoney, K. T., & Cogliser, C. C. (2010). Scholarly leadership of the study of leadership: a review of *The Leadership Quarterly*'s second decade, 2000-2009. *Leadership Quarterly,* **21**(6), 922-958. doi:http://dx.doi.org/10.1016/j.leaqua.2010.10.003.

Kirkpatrick, S. A. & Locke, E. A. (1991). Leadership: do traits matter? *Executive,* **5**(2), 48-60. doi:10.5465/AME.1991.4274679

McGregor, D. (1960) *The Human Side of Emotion.* New York: McGraw-Hill

Miner, J.B (2005) *Organisational Behaviour 1 - Essential theories of motivation and leadership* New York: M.E.Sharpe, Inc

Mischel, W. (1968). *Personality and Assessment,* University of Michigan.

Northouse, P. (2015) *Introduction to Leadership.* London: Sage.

Pernecky, T. (2015) Sustainable leadership in event management. *Event Management,* **19**(1), 109-121.

Sashkin, M. & Sashkin, M. G. (2003). *Leadership that matters: the critical factors for making a difference in people's lives and organisations' success* (Vol. 18). California: Berrett-Koehler Publishers, Inc.

Stodgill, R. M. (1948). Personal factors associated with leadership: A survey of the literature. *Journal of Psychology,* **25,** 35-71.

Taylor, S. (2019). Trait theories of leaders and leadership. In Carroll, B., Ford, J. and Taylor, S. (eds) *Leadership 2,* pg 49-67, London: Sage.

Wahab, S., Shahibi, M. S., Ali, J., Bakar, S.A. & Amrin, N. A.A. (2014). The influence of leaders orientation on event management success: event crews' perception. *Social and Behavoural Sciences, 109,* 497-501

Xu, L., Fu, P., Xi, Y., Zhang, L., Zhoa, X., Cao, C., Liao, Y., Li G., Wue, X. & Ge, J. (2014) Adding dynamics to a static theory: How leader traits evolve and how they are expressed. *Leadership Quarterly,* 25: 1095-119.

Yukl, G. (2010). *Leadership in Organisations* (3rd ed.). New Jersey: Pearson.

3 Leader/follower perspectives

Chapter aims

☐ Explore and critically discuss the foundations of charismatic, transformational & transactional leadership

☐ Explore similarities and differences in the concepts of charismatic and transformational leadership

☐ Understand the key components of Leader-Member Exchange theory

☐ Consider the role of followship in leadership from a critical perspective

☐ Focus on leadership in action: transformational leadership in a DMO, by Scott Taylor.

Leader/follower perspectives – entity-relational approaches

As we saw in the previous chapter, classic approaches to understanding leadership all shared the view that leadership is a specialised role – they focused on the individual and, whilst some of these theories looked at what other influences there may be (i.e. the situational context), they did so through the lens of the primary leader, carrying out leadership functions.

This then can be seen as their one key limitation – they are leader-centric and don't tend to recognise followers' characteristics or initiatives (Uhl-Bien, Riggio, Lowe, & Carsten, 2014). This focus on the 'heroic leader' has, over the last 50 years, become increasingly criticised, as researchers began to look at leadership behaviours from a influence perspective, considering the dynamics of the leader- follower behaviours and leadership styles that might influence or change the behaviours of their followers or work subordinates. As Burns (1978) suggested, at this point, we knew a lot about leaders, whilst knowing very little about leadership. The body of work that grew out of such observations was largely concerned with what became known as charismatic and transactional / transformational leadership (Bass, 1985). Here scholars had started to focus on *leadership styles* – what is it that leaders do that makes them effective – and on the impact the leader has on their followers.

In their review of the past 25 years of leadership research, Dinh et al. (2014) note that significant research is now occurring at the dyadic level. Dyadic means the interaction between two things, so in the case of leadership we mean the interaction between the leader and the follower. This body of work predominantly emerges through studies that focus on charismatic, transformational leadership or the leader-member exchange theories. So, with the ongoing criticisms of the heroic leader theories, scholars moved into what is often known as the 'post-heroic' phase (Badaracco, 2001). It was Bass's (1985, 1995) work in particular, that started a paradigm shift from viewing leadership as something someone is, or the things someone does, or the knowledge and skills someone has, towards the notion that leadership is an influential, dyadic process (Yukl, 1999).

Since the 1980s then, the focus of leadership research has shifted towards the relational aspects of leadership, as scholars consider how interpersonal relationships inform leadership practice. This represents a significant shift from the pure entity approaches to leadership studies, as described in Chapter 2 (i.e. those studies that focus on leadership as something someone special 'does') and those that look at the individual's interpersonal relationships, as described in this chapter (i.e. those studies that look at how leadership exists within relationships between two people – the leader, and the follower).

The overriding purpose of this chapter is to articulate the background to the current arguments existing in the literature, which suggest that leadership is too often reduced to a dyadic, influential, one-way (top-down) relationship and to highlight how these entity-relational perspectives are still predominant in event studies.

Charismatic leadership

From theories such as the trait or Great Man theory described in Chapter 2, the notion that charisma is an essential element of leadership emerged. Weber (1947) is widely credited with suggesting that charisma is a special kind of leadership trait, which helped to see people through times of crisis. Charismatic leaders, Weber suggested, emerged during periods of crisis with radical views that attracted followers. Whilst Weber is often credited as being the founder of charismatic leadership, it wasn't until the mid-1970s that it was developed in an organisational context. Key writers here include Bryman (1992), Conger (1989) and Conger and Kanungo (1987, 1998).

For these later scholars, charismatic leadership was broadly viewed through three different lenses (Schedlitzki & Edwards, 2018). The first was those who took a behavioural view of charismatic leadership, and suggested that charismatic leaders could be identified through what they did, and how they behaved (e.g. Bryman suggested charismatic leaders would be great orators). The second was those that viewed charisma as something that the followers bestowed on the leader, and therefore became highly committed to them (e.g. Conger and Kanaungo, 1987, 1998). The third view of charismatic leadership takes a relational perspective, suggesting that charismatic leadership is dependent on the relationship between leader and follower, and is based on shared ideological values.

The issue with charismatic leadership is that often leaders are chosen at a time when there is a problem that needs solving, or deep-rooted unhappiness. In other words, when we are in uncertain times, we are more likely to seek out leadership from charismatic leaders – those 'heroic' leaders, who have the charisma (which often implies the nerve or daring) to bring about the change people think they need. This may well be why we have seen Donald Trump and Boris Johnson elected to run countries at a time of clear uncertainty and disruption – their charisma entertains us, and it makes us feel good at a time when feeling good is in scant supply. They are leading through conviction – the conviction that their 'new' way is better than the one that has gone before – and with charisma, to convince the voting public that they are the same as them. Of course, these leaders do inevitably fail – when times get really tough (see for example the Corona virus pandemic) then charismatic leaders, and their single mindedness and conviction that they are always right, do not have the ability to bring people together and empower a collaborative response. (For an interesting discussion on Boris Johnson and the problem with charismatic leadership, see Stern & Stokes, 2019, 2020.)

Charismatic leadership then is the idea that people follow leaders because of their personality, their attractiveness or because of the vision they are providing. In order for the leader to be successful, they must transform the followers' values and beliefs. There is some confusion between the terms used here – lots of textbooks suggest that charismatic and transformational leadership are the same thing. However, when you look closely, you can see that transformational leadership tends to be defined with a larger scope that charismatic leadership. For example, Bass (1985) took the early theories of charismatic leadership, and advanced it – his work found that charisma was one component of a larger concept of leadership, called transformational leadership. We'll explore that next.

Transactional and transformational leadership

Bass, and other scholars using his foundational work, began to look beyond the individual and to view leadership as a process that can be seen in the relationship between leaders and followers. This are known as transformational and transactional leadership theories (Bass, 1985, 1995).

In early research by Burns (1978), leadership was defined as inducing followers to pursue common, or at least joint, purposes. These purposes represented the values and motivations of both the leader, and the follower. Burns distinguished between two types of leadership – transactional leadership and transforming leadership (later changed to transformational leadership). It is generally agreed that there are five dimensions of transformational leadership and three dimensions of transactional leadership. These are sometimes known as the four I's and can be described as distinct behaviours. These have been widely summarised in literature, and I do so again here, using Judge & Piccolo (2004) as my main guide:

Transactional leadership dimensions
Contingent reward
The leader obtains agreements from the follower on what needs to be done, and offers bonuses or recognition if they meet these goals. The reward is *contingent* on the follower meeting the goals set by the leader
Management-by-exception - active
The leader only intervenes and starts to manage when the followers do not meet the set goals, or performance targets. In the active management-by-exception, the leader is actively evaluating performance of followers and watch carefully for mistakes, taking corrective action when necessary.
Management-by-exception – passive
As in active action, the leader only intervenes when the followers do not meet set goals. But passive leaders will wait for mistakes to occur – passively assessing the work after it has finished and only then taking corrective action.
Transformational leadership dimensions
Idealised influence (charisma)
The leader is a strong role model and leads by example. They recognise followers' needs, and prioritise them.
Inspirational motivation
The leader inspires their followers to achieve, through shared visions and goals for their organisation. They inspire commitment.
Intellectual stimulation
The leader encourages the follower to think for themselves. They create learning opportunities for their followers.
Individualised consideration
The leader establishes strong relationships with their followers. They behave in caring and supportive ways.

Table 3.1: Transactional and transformational leadership dimensions

Transactional leadership

Transactional leadership involves an exchange or transaction between leader and follower. These exchanges involve direction and specific requirements from the leader, with personal rewards if the follower successfully completed a task and punishments if they do not (Bass & Bass, 2008; Rosenbach & Taylor, 2006). Transactional leaders are typically defined as those who ensure that their followers are able to clearly understand the role they need to play in achieving an organisation's outcomes and in order to be rewarded; and are reactionary, taking action when things aren't going to plan. In addition, transactional leaders take the values, needs and motivations of followers as being static and unchanging. Transactional leadership is therefore focussed on self-interest and as such, it is often considered as managerial leadership (Rosenbach & Taylor, 2006). Refer back to Chapter 1 for that discussion on the difference between management and leadership if you need clarification here.

Consider the nature of mega sporting events such as the Olympics, which involve using vast numbers of volunteers to support the delivery of the event. Why do these people volunteer, what do they get out of it? Research shows that they are either intrinsically motivated or extrinsically motivated. Alexander et al., (2015) describe the volunteering process as the formation of a symbiotic, mutually beneficial relationship which, if done correctly, will ensure ongoing support. Their research found that the London 2012 volunteers were motivated by things like opportunities to strengthen skills and develop professional networks or to improving mental health, happiness and community development. So for LOCOG (the London 2012 organising committee) it was fairly easy to establish what the volunteers wanted to get out of their time working at the event, and to harness those needs in order to motivate this unpaid workforce. Future Olympic organising committees can take this understanding of why people volunteer and build it into their recruitment and training – and this would be a clear form of transactional leadership. Indeed, in a study of staff working at the 2014 FIFA World cup and the 2016 Olympic games, Megheirkouni (2018) found that transactional leadership was used more often than transformational leadership at both events.

Similarly, Parent, Beaupre and Seguin (2009) and Parent, Olver and Seguin (2009) used data from the World Aquatics Championships and the LPC scale to identify which of leadership style is the most appropriate for a sporting event. They concluded that transformational leadership is difficult in sporting events because of the reliance on volunteers and the associated lack of time to give them the attention transformational leadership required. They argue, therefore, that transactional leadership is more effective because, whilst there is no monetary reward for volunteers, transactional leaders can reward with other incentives. We'll return to this point later.

Transformational leadership

Transformational leadership involves motivating and influencing followers to excel. Transformational leaders allow followers to see and understand the overall objectives of a task; they provide a shared vision that motivates their followers to move beyond self-interest and ensures that followers' self-esteem and self-actualisation needs are satisfied (Bass, 1995). Transformational leaders therefore view the values, needs and motivations of followers as changeable and they are able to motivate their followers to do more than they originally expected to do.

In transformational leadership, leaders are also role models, setting an example and ensuring that followers understand the shared assumptions, beliefs and values (Rosenbach & Taylor, 2006). The effects of transformational leadership are "...*follower motivation, commitment and trust, respect and loyalty to the leader*" (Dionne et al., 2014, p. 12). The result then is a positive relationship which ultimately results in followers being more motivated to work harder, and to accept further leadership.

In his key work on transformational leadership, Bass (1985) found that it consisted of three factors – the charismatic leadership described in the first section of this chapter, intellectual stimulation and individualised consideration. For Bass, successful transformational leaders are not just charismatic leaders – they are able to intellectually stimulate their followers by providing them with an awareness of the problems in the workplace, and how those problems might be solved and they give individuals personal attention so that each follower is treated individually, and each follower can get what he or she wants.

Returning to those sporting mega events, and the vast numbers of staff and volunteers to plan and deliver them – can these mega events help us to understand transformational leadership better as well? Treating all those staff members as individuals, and ensuring that each person gets what they want seems like an almost impossible task. But the Olympics' is not run by one person – it is a large assortment of individual organisations and teams, each operating semi-independently. And within each of these teams, staff and volunteers must be empowered to accomplish the overall event goal. Megheirkouni's research found that leaders were more likely to use transformational leadership when goals needed to be met, and transactional leadership to ensure orders were followed.

Transformational leadership and transactional leadership are not necessarily mutually exclusive (Pearce et al., 2002) – studies have demonstrated how leaders can use both, with people moving between both styles of leadership, depending on what the situation calls for. This suggests that people are not either transformational leaders or transactional leaders, but can actually be both – and the situation can help leaders to decide if the follower needs the carrot (transforming, motivational leadership) or the stick (transactional, exchange driven leadership).

Transformational leadership theories are still one of the most popular today – numerous studies are published every year, and whilst much of the event research has yet to focus on leadership, there are one or two that focus on event tourism. For example, in research by Schofield et al. (2018), transformational leadership was found to play a key part in Glasgow City Marketing Bureau's management strategies. In particular, they noted that long-term, extensive, collaborative stakeholder engagement enacted through transformational leadership was one of the critical success factors for the destination marketing organisation (DMO).

There is significant, empirically proven, evidence to support the use of transformational theories. Studies have found significant relationships between transformational leadership and the amount of effort followers are willing to exert, the satisfaction with the leader and with the perceived effectiveness of the transformational leadership. Events students wishing to further their understanding of transformational leadership would do well to start their research in the related fields of tourism and hospitality, where there topic has received a fair amount of scholarly attention. In addition, the theory has gained popularity in practice too – there are a number of training courses within the event industry that use the theory to train new event managers.

However, as interesting and useful as transformational leadership has been shown to be, it is still does not paint the full picture of leadership that is needed these days. And that is simply because the basic unit of analysis – the focus for nearly all of these studies – is on what the leader does, and how the leader's interactions impact on the follower. It therefore neglects both the situation in which leadership takes place, and relegates the followers to the position of passive reception of leadership. But surely those that follow have some influence too?

Followship in leadership studies

Throughout the book so far, you might have noticed the use of the term followers and wondered why I use that term, rather than subordinate or employee. The answer is that, in leadership theory, followers or followship is used as a term that implies a willingness to accept direction and guidance from leaders. The term recognises that for organisations to be effective, they need both those that lead, and those that follow. It therefore recognises that the leader and the follower both have important roles to play in the process of leadership. In events, and other service industries, being an effective follower is seen as an important element for achieving service-orientated goals, as teams of employees work to plan and deliver events in a timely and satisfactory manner. In planned events, followers often have to work independently of the formal leader, and carry out important tasks – and they do so in an active, participatory role, in which the follower willingly takes on responsibility for delivering the events successfully. Service industries such as ours are highly reliant on staff who need to be trained and knowledgeable about brands, about the events and about how to meet and exceed guest expectations in a consistent manner (Deale et al., 2016).

Chaleff (1995, 2008) identified five qualities for followship

♦   The courage to assume responsibility

♦   The courage to serve

♦   The courage to challenge

♦   The courage to participate in personal and organisational transformation

♦   The courage to take moral action.

When we consider the management and delivery of planned events and event tourism, we can see that each of these qualities is important for an event manager.

Followship has gained more scholarly attention in recent years, and we'll explore some of the most popular emerging theories (and some of the criticisms of the theory) in Chapter 4. However, the idea that the relationship between leader and follower is central to successful leadership is not new. In fact, the type and quality of this relationship has long been considered as important in some areas of leadership study. In particular, scholars argued that theories such as transformational leadership forgot that there cannot be leaders without followers back in the late 1990s, and in doing so promoted the development of leadership theories such as the Leader-Member Exchange.

Leader-Member Exchange (LMX)

Whilst transformational leadership studies abound, the concept is not without its critics – Yukl (1999, 2012) is one of the leading critical voices and, throughout his scholarly career, he noted a number of issues. In particular, he notes that much of the research into transformational leadership exists at the dyadic level, and fails to take into account the process of influence that is required at both the group level and the organisational level. He notes that "...[at group level] the core transformational behaviours should probably include facilitating agreement about objectives and strategies, facilitating mutual trust and cooperation and building group identification and collective efficacy" (Yukl, 1999, p. 290). He also notes that transformational leadership behaviours are nearly always analysed only at the individual level, but that th ey should also be analysed at the organisational level, with scholars expanding the existing studies to also look for articulations of a vision and strategy for the organisation, and leaders that guide and facilitate change and promote organisational learning. Yukl first noted this in 1999, and since then scholars have begun to develop theories that incorporate or build on transformational behaviours but also include wider behaviours and multi-level research that attempts to clarify the nature of the influence process. A leader-member exchange (LMX) perspective is one of these key theoretical developments, which has increased in popularity over the last 20 years.

In the late 1970s and 1980s, researchers began to find that leaders needed to influence more than just their followers; they also needed to influence their own managers, peers and external stakeholders (Kaplan, 1984; Mintzberg, 1973). This viewpoint was, in effect, a criticism of the transformational leadership style theories; researchers in those areas were not sufficiently concerned with the influence process and the actions or interactions of other team members. One key response to emerge from this criticism is the leader-member exchange theory (Dansereau et al., 1975) and its precursor, the vertical dyad linkage model. Unlike transformational leadership, LMX theory suggests that leaders do not treat all subordinates the same – instead, they develop an exchange with their direct reports, and it is the quality of that exchange that influences performance and effectiveness (Dionne et al., 2014; Graen & Uhl-Bien, 1995a). This body of work therefore shifts the focus from specific leadership styles towards the view that leadership is an influence process, in which relationships matter. It doesn't, however, stray far from the dominant discourse in leadership studies because the focus is still on what the leader does and how the leader treats those following them.

In LMX, the domains of leadership therefore consist of leader, follower and relationship (Graen & Uhl-Bien, 1995a), and leadership is viewed *"…as a process whereby an individual influences a group of individuals to achieve a common goal"* (Northouse, 2017, p. 7). The central proposition in LMX then is that leaders differentiate the way they treat their followers through the formation of different types of work-related exchanges. Leaders may not treat all members of the team the same, and it is the quality of this differentiation, which is known as the LMX differentiation (Liden et al., 2006), that matters to LMX.

Higher quality, or strong, LMX relationships refer to social exchanges that go beyond the requirements of the formal employment contracts – followers who benefit from these high-quality exchanges are sometimes referred to as the 'in-group'. In these high quality exchange relationships, leaders and followers show levels of mutual loyalty, respect, trust, affection and obligation (Dulebohn et al., 2012; Graen, 2003). They may also offer mentoring and empowerment in exchange for increased commitment to completing non-contracted tasks and better quality task performance from their subordinates (Liden et al., 2006). Research has demonstrated that when there is a high quality LMX between leader and follower, a number of valuable outcomes occur, including improved job performance, satisfaction, commitment, role clarity and decreased turnover intentions (Gertsner & Day, 1997).

Research has also demonstrated that when there is a high quality of LMX relationship, employees feel obliged to reciprocate through an equally valued exchange (see review by Ilies, Nahrgang & Morgeson, 2007) – this common rule of reciprocity is based on social exchange theory and suggests that the member must 'pay back' the leader through hard work. In addition, these positive exchanges ensure that the follower increasingly likes the leader, which leads to motivation to complete the leader's work demands (Martin et al., 2016). Low quality LMX relations – or the 'out-group' are characterised by contractual exchanges that do not progress beyond the realms of the agreed employment (Sparrowe & Liden, 1997).

In research into stadia and arenas hosting events, Megheirkouni (2017) looked at the mediating impacts of leader-member exchange theory on the relationship between job satisfaction, organisational commitment and performance of staff. Findings indicated that, when employees experienced high quality LMX, they are more likely to show a high-level of commitment to their work and a high level of performance. In addition, job satisfaction was positively and directly related to job per-formance, as well as organisational commitment. So LMX certainly has some positive use in hosting sports events – it is perhaps likely to also be useful in other events of similar size, scale and activity.

Other advantages of LMX theory are that leaders can look at their own leadership and evaluate the relationships they have formed, in order to recognise if they are favouring some staff and bypassing others – in other words, they can use it to recognise the out-group and the in-group. In addition, it allows for the training, mentoring and develop-ment of staff who are in the out-group, to move them into the in-group – research shows that those with high quality relationships are motivated and more productive (Graen, 2003; Graen & Uhl-Bien, 1995a; Graen & Uhl-Bien, 1995b; Kramer, 2006). So it allows formal leaders to put the right people in the right place at the right time.

Criticisms of the LMX theory centre around issues with the range of measures available to identify LMX, many of which don't tend to justify why changes have been made from previous measures already avail-able. Other criticisms are that it focuses too much on the relationship and not enough on the leadership behaviours. In addition, the theory of LMX was originally developed to try to account for the differentiating behaviours of leaders with multiple followers, to see how this differen-tiation may influence activities within a work group (Henderson et al., 2009). It is odd then that the majority of research is still conducted at the dyadic level, with little empirical work that examines LMX at group level giving little scope to understand if LMX differentiation can influence other relationships in a group.

A final – and persuasive – criticism of LMX theory is that there is a failure to consider the social contexts in which the leaders and followers are necessarily embedded. To date, there has been little investigation into whether specific contexts account for significant variances in practice, or whether the organisational context might impact on the quality of the LMX relationships (Dulebohn et al., 2012). So, despite a move towards a more complex view of leadership, LMX theory provides little understanding about the lived experience of these exchanges. As scholars focussed on the social exchanges within organisational relationships, they began to question why research focussed solely on the relationship between leader and follower. Also, remember that, whilst LMX theory has shifted the research focus away from what individual leaders do, the focus is still very much on the dyadic relationships and influence processes between leaders and followers.

Summary

This chapter has sought to establish that research has, for the most part, taken an entity approach to leadership, with leadership viewed solely through the lens of the primary leader or, more recently, through the perspective of the relationships the leader has with subordinates, and with a focus on leadership styles. This is problematic because when leadership is viewed only through the lens of what one formal leader does, it neglects both the context of leadership processes and the abilities of others within teams, organisations and networks to take leadership roles. Leadership is rarely the preserve of just a single individual, but tends to be undertaken by multiple individuals in a team, and responsibilities tend to lie with those individuals whose expertise most closely matches the needs of the task.

In more recent studies, however, there has been a move towards an expanded understanding of leadership with research moving into discussions around how and where leadership is constructed and who or what is contributing to that relationship. Badaracco (2001) describes this as a 'post-heroic' phase – and this represents a significant shift in theory, in which scholars now consider that the centre of leadership is not just found in the role of the formal leader, but is also found in the interaction of team members to lead the team by sharing leadership responsibilities. There is, therefore, a growing body of research that convincingly argues that leadership is relational and multi-level, which involves leaders, followers, and the social influence processes of larger networks. This body of work is explored in detail in the next chapter.

Leadership in action: Industry insight from Scott Taylor, CEO, Advance City Marketing and former CEO of Glasgow City Marketing Bureau

Scott Taylor has led Glasgow's remarkable growth in tourism, conventions and major events for almost 20 years. As founding CEO of the city's first Destination Marketing Organisation, Glasgow City Marketing Bureau, the company celebrated winning M&It Best UK Convention Bureau for ten consecutive years. The city secured £1.2billion in revenue in just ten years, averaging 500 conference wins per year. In 2015, Glasgow achieved its best ICCA world ranking of conference destinations at 24th. This experience combines with success in bidding for major events, including UEFA Champions League, UEFA Euro 2020, 2014 Commonwealth Games and MTV Europe Music Awards. Scott was on the bid team that developed the bid for the 2014 Commonwealth Games, and was on the final pitch team in Colombo for the successful pitch. He was awarded an Honorary Doctorate for serves to tourism and the economy from Glasgow Caledonian University in 2016 and is now CEO of Advance City Marketing, advising national and local government on strategy for DMOs.

Destination Marketing Organisations (DMOs) are largely strategic organisations, acting on behalf of a wide range of partnerships and acting as catalysts and conduits for the transfer of the value of events and tourism to those partnerships.

I think being able to harness people's creativity and enthusiasm is the trick of leadership. Good leadership is when leaders are able to deliver great change and also are prepared to change and to exit when the time is right. To lead and leave your organisation, means you have to bring your team on, and make yourself as redundant as you possibly can. And if you work on the basis that you are not going to be the leader forever, then you are prepared to take risks, to try to achieve something significant – and if it goes badly wrong, that's my signature on that and if it goes wonderfully well – it's my signature on that too. So risk taking is the most important principal that leaders should do. Take more risks. There is more to leadership than that of course – but if you fear change, then you will never lead a changing, dynamic organisation. You can't do it if you are afraid. Also creating a feeling of stability and fairness in the organisation goes a long way to creating commitment and loyalty to the organisation. And commitment and loyalty from team members shouldn't be viewed as out of date – those values are often under-rated.

Ultimately the role of the destination marketing agency is to create jobs and employment on a massive, industrial scale. This meant that, in Glasgow, we had to leverage a lot of partnership activity, in order to drive demand and create the need for work within the city. In the DMO, everything you do is around creating demand, stimulating supply and supporting supply growth, which ultimately creates a jobs growth – so that then creates a single vision, that you embody within the organisation. So our mission was to create customers, in order to create jobs. We were aiming to create employment opportunities for people who don't work, can't work or who have never worked and who should have access to work as a human right. So everyone in the organisation knew that they were doing good, and they knew their work had a purpose. And of course everyone knew someone who couldn't get a job, was unemployed or was struggling to find employment – and this became a really easy mantra that people could remember – we create customers to create jobs. So our employees knew what they were doing was making a significant difference.

Setting a vision and a mission was a conscious decision. We involved the whole of our team within Glasgow City Marketing Bureau, a team of 67 employees. That mission also translated into a cultural mission for us. When people come to work, they bring their culture with them – if they are having a bad day, they will bring that to work.

And very often, cultures at work aren't very well defined, and they are not described. We described the kind of place that we wanted to work in, which makes a really refreshing way of setting your organisation's daily values. So alongside the usual things you have when establishing a culture – such as accountability – which can translate into saying what you do, and doing what you say, we simplify it and make it so everyone understands it – making it clear that, as management, we will do that too – we can't just say we are going to do something, and then not do it. So we can't just say we are going to treat everyone fairly and equally, we need to show our strategies for doing that, how are you going to demonstrate that you are doing that? Our cultural mission was the essence of the organisation. So we decided we would be a very creative organisation, and to do that, we set up a real culture of risk taking and innovation so that effectively it was 'what have we done that is new today, that is just different, just better' – excellence comes through the building of tiny, incremental points of difference. If you are only doing one a week, or one a month it won't be enough. You need to do it as part of your daily routine.

Study questions

1   What is the key difference between entity perspectives of leadership presented in Chapter 2 and the dyadic perspectives discussed here?

2   Do you think that relationships matter in leadership? If not, why not? And if so, why?

3   Have you experienced charismatic or transformational leadership in the workplace? If so, describe the strengths and weaknesses from your perspective.

4   Why would transformational leadership be particularly useful in an events setting?

5   Can you think of situations during the event planning and event delivery process in which transactional leadership might be a useful tool for an event manager to use?

6   This chapter has been quite critical of LMX theories of leadership. What do you think? Can you see it being useful in your future career?

7 After reading the Leadership in Action section, how would you describe Scott's leadership style?

Further reading

Bass, B. M. (1995). Theory of transformational leadership redux. *The Leadership Quarterly,* 6: 463-478.

Bryman, A. (1992) *Charisma and Leadership in Organisations*. London: Sage.

Parry, K. And Kempser, S. (2014) Love and leadership: constructing follower narrative identities of charismatic leadership. *Management Learning*, **45**, 21-38.

Conger, J.A. (2011) Charismatic jeadership. In Bryman, A., Collinson, D., Grint, K., Jackson, B. & Uhl-Bien, M. (eds) *The SAGE Handbook of Leadership*, pp. 86-102. London: Sage.

Megheirkouni, M. (2017). Revisting leader-member exchange theory: insights into stadia management. *International Journal of Event and Festival Management, 8*(3), 244-260.

Tourish, D. (2013) *The Dark Side of Transformational Leadership: A critical perspective*. Hove, UK: Routledge.

References

Alexander, A., Kim, S.B. & Kim, D.Y. (2015) Segmenting volunteers by motivation in the 2012 London Olympic Games. *Tourism Management*, **47**, 1-10.

Badaracco, J. (2001). We don't need another hero. *Harvard Business Review*, *79*(8), 120-126.

Bass, B. M. (1985). *Leadership and Performance Beyond Expectations*. New York: The Free Press.

Bass, B. M. (1995). Theory of transformational leadership redux. *Leadership Quarterly*, **6**(4), 463-478.

Bass, B. M. & Bass, R. (2008). *The Bass Handbook of Leadership: Theory, research & managerial applications* (4th ed.). New York: Free Press.

Bryman, A. (1992) *Charisma and Leadership in Organisations*. London: Sage.

Burns, J. (1978) *Leadership*. New York: Harper Row.

Chaleff, I. (1995). *The Courageous Follower: Standing up to and for our leaders*. San Francisco,CA: Barrett-Koehler Publishers, Inc.

Chaleff, I. (2008). Creating new ways of following. The art of followership: how great followers create great leaders and organizations. In Riggio, R. E., Chaleff, I., & Lipman-Blumen, J.(Eds.). *The Art of Followership: How great followers create great leaders and organizations.* (1st ed., pp. 67-87). San Francisco, CA: Jossey Bass.

Conger, J.A. (1989) *The Charismatic Leader: Behind the Mystique of Exceptional Leadership.* San Francisco, CA: Jossey-Bass

Conger, J.A. & Kanungo, R.N. (1987) Toward a behavioural theory: Charismatic leadership in organisational settings. *Academy of Management Review,* **12**: 637-647.

Conger, J.A. & Kanungo, R.N. (1998) *Charismatic Leadership in Organisations.* Thousand Oaks, CA: Sage.

Dansereau, F., Graen, G. & Haga, W. (1975). A vertical dyad linkage approach to leadership within formal organisations: a longitudinal investigation of the role-making process. *Organisational Behaviour and Human Performance,* 13, 46-78.

Deale, C.S. Shoffstall, D.G. & Brown, E.A. (2016) What does it mean to follow? An exploration of a followship profile in hospitality and tourism. *Journal of Teaching in Travel and Tourism,* **16**(4) 235-252.

Dinh, J., Lord, R.G., Gardner, W.L., Meuser, J.D., Liden, R.C. & Hu, J. (2014). Leadership theory and research in the new millennium: Current theoretical trends and changing perspectives. *Leadership Quarterly,* **25**(1), 36-62.

Dulebohn, J. H., Bommer, W. H., Liden, R. C., Brouer, R. L. & Ferris, G. R. (2012). A meta-analysis of antecedents and consequences of Leader-Member Exchange. *Journal of Management,* **38**(6), 1715-1759. doi:10.1177/0149206311415280.

Gertsner, C. R. & Day, D. V. (1997). Meta-analytic review of leader-member exchange theory: correlates and construct issues. *Journal of Applied Psychology,* **82**(6), 827-844.

Graen, G. (2003). Role making onto the starting work team using LMX leadership: diversity as an asset. In G. Graen (Ed.), *New Frontiers of Leadership* (pp. 33-66). Greenwich: Information Age.

Graen, G. & Uhl-Bien, M. (1995a). Development of Leader-Member exchange theory of leadership over 25 years: applying a multi-domain perspective. *Leadership Quarterly,* **6**(2), 219-247.

Graen, G. B. & Uhl-Bien, M. (1995b). Relationship-based approach to leadership: Development of leader-member exchange (LMX) theory of leadership over 25 years: Applying a multi-level multi-domain perspective. *Leadership Quarterly, 6*(2), 219-247. doi:10.1016/1048-9843(95)90036-5.

Henderson, D. J., Liden, R. C., Glibkowski, B. C. & Chaudry, C. (2009). LMX Differentiation: A multilevel review and examination of its antecedents and outcomes. *Leadership Quarterly, 20*(2), 517-534.

Ilies, R., Nahrgang, J. & Morgeson, F. (2007). Leader-member exchange and citizenship behaviours: a meta-analysis. *Journal of Applied Psychology, 92*, 269-277.

Judge, T.A. & Piccolo, R.F. (2004) Transformational and transactional leadership: A meta-analytic test of their relative validity. *Journal of Applied Psychology. 80*(5), 755-768.

Kaplan, R. E. (1984). Trade routes: The manager's network of relationships. *Organisational Dynamics, 12*(4), 37-52.

Kramer, M. W. (2006). Communication strategies for sharing leadership within a creative team: LMX in theatre groups. In G. Graen & J. A. Graen (Eds.), *Sharing Network Leadership*. USA: IPA.

Liden, R. C., Erdogan, B., Wayne, S. J. & Sparrowe, R. T. (2006). Leader-Member exchange, differentiation and task interdependence: implications for individuals and group performance. *Journal of Organisational Behaviour, 27*(6), 723-746.

Martin, R., Guillaume, Y., Thomas, G., Lee, A. & Epitropaki, O. (2016). Leader–Member Exchange (LMX) and performance: a meta-analytic review. *Personnel Psychology, 69*(1), 67-121. doi:10.1111/peps.12100.

Megheirkouni, M. (2017). Revisiting leader-member exchange theory: insights into stadia management. *International Journal of Event and Festival Management, 8*(3), 244-260.

Megheirkouni, M. (2018). Leadership and decision-making styles in large scale sporting events. *Event Management, 22*, 785-801.

Mintzberg, H. (1973). The Nature of Managerial Work. New York: Harper & Row.

Northouse, P. (2017). *Introduction to Leadership: Concepts and practice*. Thousand Oaks, CA: Sage.

Parent, M., Beaupre, R. & Seguin, B. (2009). Key leadership qualities for major sporting events: The case of the World Aquatics Championships. *International Journal of Sport Management and Marketing, 6*(4), 367-388.

Parent, M., Olver, D. & Seguin, B. (2009). Understanding leadership in major sporting events: The case of the 2005 World Aquatics Championships. *Sports Management Review,* **12**(3), 167-184.

Pearce, C.L., Sims, H.P. & Cox, J.F. (2002) *Can a leader be both transactional and transformational? An empirical analysis using latent class modelling.* Working paper, Claremont Graduate University, Claremont, CA.

Rosenbach, W. E. & Taylor, R. L. (2006*). Contemporary Issues in Leadership* (6th ed.). Boulder, Colorado: Westview Press.

Schedlitzki, D. & Edwards, G. (2018) *Studying Leadership: Traditional and critical approaches.* 2nd Ed. London: Sage.

Schofield, P., Crowther, P., Jago, L., Heeley, K. & Taylor, S., (2018) Collaborative innovation: catalyst for a destination's event success. *International Journal of Contemporary Hospitality Management,* 30(6) 2499-2518.

Sparrowe, R. T. & Liden, R. C. (1997). Process and structure in Leader-Member Exchange. *Academy of Management Review,* **22**(2), 522-552. doi:10.2307/259332.

Stern, J. & Stokes, S. (2019) Why Britain should be aware of charismatic leaders offering Brexit solutions. *The Conversation,* 8th May. https://theconversation.com/why-britain-should-beware-of-charismatic-leaders-promising-easy-brexit-solutions-116677.

Stern, J. & Stokes, S. (2020) Boris Johnson needs to show a 'post-heroic' style of leadership now. *The Conversation,* April 27. https://theconversation.com/boris-johnson-needs-to-show-a-post-heroic-style-of-leadership-now-137299

Uhl-Bien, M., Riggio, R., Lowe, K. B. & Carsten, M. K. (2014). Followership Theory: a review and research agenda. *Leadership Quarterly,* 25(1), 83-104.

Weber, M. (1947) *The Theory of Social and Economic Organisations.* New York: Free Press.

Yukl, G. (1999). An evaluation of conceptual weaknesses in transformational and charismatic leadership theories. *Leadership Quarterly,* **10**(2), 285-305.

Yukl, G. (2012). Effective leadership behaviour: what we know and what questions need more attention. *Academy of Management Perspectives,* **26**(4), 66.

4 The new wave of leadership studies

Chapter aims

- ☐ Introduce and critically examine the concepts of moral leadership and the role of the 'new heroes'
- ☐ Critically discuss the behaviours of an ethical leader, and the benefits of ethical leadership for service encounters
- ☐ Examine the concept of authentic leadership, and what it means to be a just and honest leader
- ☐ Introduce and critically discuss servant leadership, and its potential to improve service encounters in the event industry
- ☐ Focus on leadership in action: learning how to be a leader by Melissa Noakes.

The new wave of moral leadership studies

In their comprehensive review of leadership research, Dionne et al. (2014) identify 29 different thematic categories of leadership theories, developed over 100 years; 17 are 'classic' leadership categories, and 12 are classified as emerging. Dinh et al. (2014) note seven emerging theories in their review and in their examination of recent theoretical and empirical developments, while Avolio, Walumbwa and Weber (2009) note 13 significant areas of new inquiry into leadership. These studies indicate that there has been a focus shift in leadership studies, which represents a diversification of thinking around how leadership occurs, and what leadership actually is. In particular, scholars have begun to focus on the moral nature of leaders, suggesting that leaders now need to be concerned with issues of ethics and morality (Lemoine, Hartnell & Leroy, 2019).

This shift in leadership studies can be partially attributed to a number of very public corporate and government scandals, financial crises and economic downturns. Cases such as the 2001 Enron scandal, in which the company executives fraudulently concealed large financial losses in certain projects and the 2008 Lehmann Brothers and Northern Rock collapses have created an interest in how leaders can enhance employee loyalty and commitment to their organisations, and how to foster cooperative aptitudes among employees (Hassan et al., 2013). Scholars have therefore started to focus on the ethical and moral behaviours of leaders. This has resulted in three emerging forms of 'positive' leadership studies – authentic leadership, ethical leadership and servant leadership. These are sometimes described as responsible or moral leadership – or, as Yammarino (2013) puts it, theories of the 'new hero'. These 'moral' forms of leadership focus on leader behaviours that are ethical, moral, professional and socially responsible. They suggest that the leader's interpersonal dynamics will increase the followers' confidence and motivate them to perform better than is expected.

Authentic, ethical and servant leadership perspectives are conceptually closely related both to each other, and to the field of transformational leadership, with a recent meta-analysis suggested that authentic and ethical leadership, and to some degree servant leadership, were all in fact incremental variances of transformational leadership (Hoch et al., 2018). However, these new theories have been developed beyond transformational leadership in that they now acknowledge that transformational leaders can also be unethical, abusive or self-serving.

Ethical leadership

Ethical leadership is leadership that emphasises the leader's ethical standards. Ethical leaders do the right thing.

Business practice has shifted over the last few years, and for many organisations in the event industry, existing purely for profit has been replaced with a triple bottom line approach that seeks to meet commercial objectives whilst also trying to do social good and reduce environmental harm. Responsible business practice in the industry is therefore becoming increasingly important, as consumers select their leisure time activities based on the organisation's ethical stance on things like contributing to society and sustainability. As consumers have become more conscientious about the events they attend, and the potential damage they can do, they have started to demand greater transparency from event organisations on how they operate. We can see this most clearly in areas such as environmental management – due to consumer demand, most event organisations now ensure they have an environmental policy, and that they are transparent in how they manage things like waste and plastic. This then has led to organisations thinking about their ethical stance, and has created a new brand of leadership, that of ethical leadership.

Ethical leaders seek to do the right thing, and conduct both their lives and their leadership roles in an ethical manner. They are guided by ethical beliefs and values, and they engage in acts and behaviours that benefit others, whilst refraining from behaviours that can cause any harm to others. They combine their own ethical beliefs and values with the organisational or cultural norms and they focus on complying with the external expectation created by these norms.

Ethical leaders are perceived to be moral people, setting ethical examples – they have desirable characteristics such as being trustworthy and honest and they are seen as being charismatic and fair (Brown et al., 2005). In particular they show respect for all members of their team; they listen carefully, they value all contributions and are compassionate and consider all viewpoints. They are principled decision-makers who care about the wellbeing of both their employees and the broader society. In short, ethical leadership is a combination of integrity, ethical standards and fair treatment of employees (Yukl et al., 2013).

The behaviour of an ethical leader is likely to be associated with high-quality leader-member exchange (LMX) relationships – that's because these high-quality exchange relationships are more likely to occur when leaders are honest, trustworthy and genuinely concerned about the well-being of their followers. As such, ethical leaders are also seen to be moral managers – they proactively try to transform followers by encouraging ethical behaviour within their subordinates (Mayer et al., 2012). They influence followers to engage in ethical behaviours through behavioural modelling and transactional leadership behaviours such as rewarding, communicating and punishing (Hoch et al., 2018). We would expect ethical leaders to be very supportive and helpful when employees have a problem, fair when distributing rewards and benefits, and open and honest in their communications. They will set clear ethical standards for the work, which focuses on the importance of their stated values. They will also hold people to account for both ethical and unethical actions.

Research has shown that ethical leadership is associated with a number of outcomes, including motivation, satisfaction and improved performance of employees (Hassan et al., 2013). One study found that ethical leadership can result in achieving ethical work outcomes and promote innovation in service organisations such as tourist hotels (Dhar, 2016). This suggests that ethical leadership can help improve service innovation and therefore service quality for industries like the events sector and, given the damage the recent Covid-19 pandemic created for the event industry, there is an urgent need for innovative high-quality service to ensure the industry recovers.

Event businesses that are perceived to be ethical can attract more volunteers, recruit better staff and increase turnover. This is evident in the increased use of corporate social responsibility strategies, which often take place at corporate events (see for example Cisco, who helped the charity Stop Hunger Now package more than 100,000 meals for the hungry during its CISCO Live event in 2015). And some event business build their entire business on ethical credentials – these can be charitable event management organisations such as Jane Tomlinson's Run for All, or social enterprise organisations, that use commercial business practice to meet specific social objectives. An example of a social enterprise is Big Bright Star (bigbrightstar.com) who are a Scottish event management company focused exclusively on running events with a social purpose and creating positive social change. Another is Tickets for Good (ticketsforgood.co.uk) who use ticket sales to create donation programmes within the event industry for charities and social projects. Their organisational mission is to support the improvement of health and well-being and to increase access to events. These two organisations have ethical leadership at the heart of everything that they do.

And event businesses can also build their entire model on unethical behaviours – see for example the now infamous Fyre Festival, which brought into sharp focus some of the darker ethical issues within the event industry. The festival was billed as an exclusive, luxury event, and was launched with a huge influencer campaign enacted on social media. Some of the influencers – including Kendall Jenner – were reportedly paid $250,000 for Instagram posts about the festival. These Instagram posts had no mention of payment or affiliation, and looked to the general public as genuine celebrity interest. This was misleading at best, and unethical at worse. In addition, the organisers disabled comments on social media platforms, meaning that the flow of information was not transparent, and resulting in the shutting down of any dissenting voices. But the most unethical practices were only revealed after the disastrous opening weekend, in which problems with security, food, accommodation, artist relations and medical services resulted in the cancellation of the festival. The subsequent investigation resulted in one of the organisers – Billy McFarland – being sentenced to six years in prison for one count of wire fraud to defraud investors and ticket holders, and a second count to defraud a ticket vendor. Examples like this are, thankfully, rare in the event industry – but they do happen.

However, the Fyre Festival was ultimately brought down by social media revelations and the ensuing documentaries on Hulu and Netflix. This shows that, with the growth of social media, and the ease in which consumers can check organisations' actions, the need for businesses to behave ethically, and for event managers to be ethical leaders has increased. Scholars studying ethical leadership suggest that, as the importance of leadership continues to grow, organisations should try to utilise recruitment and training practices that increase the levels of ethical leadership (Mayer et al., 2012).

Authentic leadership

Authentic leadership emphasises self-awareness and being true to themselves. Authentic leaders are honest and just.

In contrast to the ethical leaders' focus on complying with external expectations, authentic leaders are primarily concerned with their own self-awareness and the importance of being authentic and truthful in interactions with others. As Avolio et al., 2004 suggest authentic leadership is best captured by the Greek philosophers who described authenticity as 'know thyself' or by Shakespeare – 'to thine own self be true'

– the essence of authentic leadership is to know, accept and remain true to one's self.

Authentic leaders are therefore *"persons who have achieved high levels of authenticity in that they know who they are, what they believe and value, and they act on those values and beliefs while transparently interacting with others"* (Avolio et al., 2004:802). These leaders have high levels of self-concordance – the goals they have set themselves align very closely with their own personal values and ethics.

The central premise is that authentic leaders will develop authenticity in followers, through increased self-awareness, self-regulation and positive modelling (Avolio & Gardner, 2005). In other words, they will be both honest and just themselves, and will demand that others are treated justly and honestly. In doing so, they will not just make their own organisations more successful, they will also play a role in improving society.

There is some overlap between authentic and ethical leadership, in that studies have shown that authentic leaders have an *internalised moral perspective* (Walumbwa et al., 2008). That means that the leader behaviour is guided by their own internal moral standards and personal values – in other words, they make decisions that are based on their core beliefs. In addition, authentic leaders behave with *relational transparency*, which means that they act in accordance with their true nature - they reveal their values and beliefs openly, and therefore says exactly what they mean (Yukl et al., 2013).

However, there are two other components to authentic leadership which are not related to ethical leadership. The first of these is *self-awareness* – a leader can be self-aware without being honest or trustworthy, and without a full understanding of their core beliefs or values. Second, the authentic leader exhibits *balanced processing* – they are objective and pragmatic in processing information and making decisions, and are highly receptive to new information and new ideas (Avolio & Gardner, 2005; Gardner et al., 2005).

So authentic leadership focuses on the leader's self-confidence, self-concept, self-awareness, authenticity and general character (Lemoine, et al., 2019). Authentic leaders are deeply aware of how they think and behave, and they are confident, hopeful, optimistic and resilient. They are also perceived to be aware of their followers' values and moral perspective, their knowledge and their strengths, and because of this, authentic leaders are able to enhance engagement, motivation, commitment and satisfaction in their employees' work (Avolio et al., 2004). Through their own authenticity, they exert influence on their followers which in turn improves their work and performance outcomes.

This use of the leader's own authenticity to improve employees' performance has been shown to have positive results in the service industry (Wang & Xie, 2019). In particular, Wang and Xie show how authentic leadership helps employees to move from intentionally putting on a false display of their emotions when serving people towards genuinely feeling the desired emotion. To put that more plainly, when the leaders are authentic in their dealings with their staff, the staff move from pretending to enjoy service encounters to really enjoying them. An example might be that, in seeing how much their leader enjoys interacting with customers, the staff become motivated to get the same responses. So, through the use of things like positive energy, job security and a safe and trusting atmosphere, the leader encourages their followers to move from pretending to be happy to see the customer, to actually feeling joy when the customer approaches. We can see then that if a leader can foster a positive environment, where staff feel that their jobs are secure and they can trust their employer, that the employees interactions with their customers will improve. So authentic leadership might well have an important role to play in service encounters in the event industry.

Servant leadership

Servant leadership emphasises the needs of the stakeholders. Servant leaders put the needs of others first, and focus on the growth and well-being of their followers and their communities.

Servant leadership has been positioned as a new field of research (Eva et al., 2019) – it was introduced in an organisational context by Greenleaf (1977), who suggested that servant leaders choose to serve first. He argues that the leader is motivated by a desire to serve and empower followers and the influence necessary for leaders is inspired by the very act of service itself (Brownell, 2010). In a review of studies in this field, van Dierendonck (2011) suggested that servant leadership is demonstrated through empowering and developing people, expressing humility and authenticity and providing direction. It is also reliant on high-quality dyadic relationships – though the focus is on the followers' needs. Relationships must therefore be based on trust and fairness and exist in a working environment that encourages positive job attitudes and has a strong organisational focus on sustainability and corporate social responsibility. Essentially, servant leaders inspire followers to become servant leaders themselves and in doing so, they improve the well-being of followers, which leads to overall effectiveness of individuals and teams.

Servant leadership is generally agreed to comprise of positive, philanthropic attributes and behaviours. Spears (2010) listed 10 characteristics of a servant leader.

1 Listening

2 Empathy

3 Healing

4 Awareness

5 Persuasion

6 Conceptualisation

7 Foresight

8 Stewardship

9 Commitment to the growth of people

10 Building community

There have only been a few studies that focus on servant leadership in events – though more can be identified in the hospitality literature (e.g. Huanget al. 2016; Wu et al., 2013). For a review of servant leadership in the hospitality industry, see Bavik, 2020. The application of servant leadership in hospitality should be very interesting to anyone studying events because of the similarities between the industries. As Bavik points out, the hospitality industry is predicated on human interaction, and 'serving' customers – this is true also of the event industry, which has service at its heart. After all, there are no events without guests. The central aim of both the hospitality and event industry is to create positive memories for their guests, and because both industries are heavily reliant on the human resource, the quality of the leader-follower relationship becomes a critical aspect of customer management.

Studies have shown that servant leadership boosts helping behaviours among employees in the hospitality industry, and reduces negative behaviours such as lateness. Servant leadership is also shown to improve the quality of the relationship between leader and follower, and thus improve employee outcomes in areas such as work engagement, work performance and work commitment. See Bavik (2020) for a summary of these studies.

In work that recognises how useful servant leadership might be in the service based event industry, Megheirkouni (2018) used a quantitative approach to identify the degree to which leaders in sports events, cultural events and personal events are perceived to be servant leaders. This extent of the servant leadership behaviours were then linked to employee job satisfaction. The findings indicated that servant leadership behaviours were adopted by managers in the context of both sporting events and personal events, but not cultural events. Findings also indicated that job satisfaction varied greatly across the sport, cultural and personal events sector. The research suggests that *"the results showed that servant leadership behaviours were not seen as being essential to the cultural events"* p.146) but, given each sample was drawn from different middle eastern countries, with the cultural events organisations being situated in Syria – we could therefore expect that leadership would be affected by the instability in the area. That criticism said, however, the work is useful and noteworthy. It is interesting to note the findings suggest that there is a positive interaction between employee job satisfaction and the servant leader's emotional behaviours.

So servant leadership consists of a set of practices that tries to build better organisations, enrich the lives of individuals and, ultimately, to create a more caring world. Servant leaders focus on the growth and well-being of the people and the communities in which they belong. They put the needs of others first, to help their followers to develop and perform as well as possible. As Getz and Page (2020) point out, this type of leadership is particularly suited for the not-for-profit sector, where events are agents of change, or are supporting the community.

This is borne out by the research of Parris and Peachey (2013) who used a longitudinal, qualitative case study to reveal that a cause-related sporting event (a charity event) encouraged servant leadership. The findings indicated that, through structural mechanisms and social processes such as building a community and creating a culture of story-telling, participants were helped to practice servant leadership. The authors argued that non-profit sporting events can therefore create sustainable communities of servant leaders.

Summary

This new wave of leadership studies attempts to build on previous scholarly understanding such as the importance of the interpersonal exchange, and leadership behaviours and – in particular – on trans-formational leadership studies. Whilst transformational leadership is leader and organisation-centred, this new wave of leadership studies are relationship-orientated. They focus on the development of good leader-follower connections.

♦ **Ethical** leadership focuses on the leader being seen to do the right thing. Ethical leaders are guided by their ethical and moral values, and by external expectations.

♦ **Authentic** leadership is sincere and transparent – authentic leaders focus on being trustworthy and honest, seeking to develop both themselves and their followers.

♦ **Servant** leadership emphasises the importance of serving others. Servant leaders prioritise the needs of the organisation, the employees, the customers and even society over their own needs.

These types of moral leadership shift the focus to the relationship between the leader and the follower. But they are still very much focussed on that one leader, in a formal leadership role. But in a modern event organisation, can we really say that the only people who 'do' leadership are those in managerial positions? Wouldn't a wide range of leadership happen when people are organising events? We'll explore this question in the next chapter.

Leadership in action: Industry insight from Melissa Noakes, co-founder of Elevate

Melissa Noakes has over 15 years' experience in the industry and has worked both agency and client-side. She has delivered world-class brand experiences for Santander, Sony Mobile, Sony, Shell, L'Oreal, Budweiser, Jack Daniels and Disney to name just a few. Melissa is the co-founder of Elevate, the UK's largest mentoring programme for the events industry, which has now helped over 400 event professionals in their career development. She is regularly cited as one of the most influential people in the UK events industry.

I remember the day I realised I was a leader. I wasn't promoted. I didn't have line management duty. I wasn't even that senior. I was leading a big event project and when something went wrong on site, everyone looked to me for the answer.

But funnily enough, the realisation that this was my first leadership experience only came when I was being mentored a few years later. By then, I had line management responsibility and I was being mentored to help with the transition into formal management. My mentor told me – and it's true – one of the biggest changes in your career development is when you go from "doing that thing you're good at" to "helping other people be good at that thing you're good at". In that same session we discussed my view of being leader and what it meant. I realised that inherently my view of 'leaders' were senior people, typically men, on stage or in charge of teams. Through my session we explored these views of leadership and I slowly realised that there were other, more subtle – but just as powerful – versions of leadership. I had been running large projects with multiple stakeholders across many areas of business, running budgets, co-ordinating deadlines, liaising with external suppliers and agencies and ensuring we met our objectives. I was leading the projects – and significant ones at that – but up until that mentoring session I had never even considered myself a leader.

In considering what makes a good leader, especially someone in an events role, I now realise there is a need for a number of key skills. First and foremost is the ability to connect with and work with lots of different types of people with differing priorities, approaches and styles and being able to influence them and bring them along with you on the journey you're going on. A leader has to have vision and be able to communicate it and empower others to deliver against it. Delegating therefore is another really key skill to learn – you simply can't do all jobs yourself and if you try to one of two things happen – you'll burn out or you disempower those around you – or worse, you do both. In delegating you need to learn how to do that both up and down the chain, for many delegating upwards is a much harder skill to learn but is critical. That mentoring session also taught me, and I continue to see evidence of this, that you are often a leader without even realising it – there are people in your professional or personal life that look up to you and look at you as a leader, right now, even without you realising.

In delivering the complex projects I have been responsible for I've learnt a lot of those skills along with being organised, learning how to manage expectations and work alongside people from the CEO, to regional leads to receptionists and PAs (who, incidentally, are the people who actually know what's happening in a business and can get you in front of senior people and are therefore critical to form good relationships with). I've also learnt to listen intently and learn from those around me, borrowing from the styles and approaches from the leaders I admire. The leaders I respect, and still do to this day, are the ones who make me feel valued, who listen to my opinions, who inspire me with their vision in a way that makes me want to give up my evenings and weekends to help bring that vision to life and the people who I actually like. I've been fortunate to have a lot of them to learn from.

Now that I am 'senior', I am a 'people manager' and I am (though I hate to admit it) 'old' I keep those lessons I learnt close to my heart. Whilst I have 20 years' experience in my field and I know many people look at me as a 'seasoned leader', I am still very much a student. I make mistakes and seek to learn from them when I do. I look to my peers and seniors to continue to grow and learn. But increasingly I look to my team and the up and coming talent and learn almost as much, if not more, from them. I don't believe you're ever fully 'finished' learning how to be a leader, but understanding you are one is the first big step on a lifetime of learning.

Study questions

1 Describe the similarities and differences between the three types of moral leadership discussed in this chapter.

2 Discuss why this new wave of moral leadership might be useful to the planning of event experiences.

3 Yammarino (2013) describes ethical, authentic and servant leaders as the new heroes. Why do you think this is?

4 There is a growing interest in servant leadership in the event industry. Why might that be?

5 How might authentic leadership improve service encounters?

6 In certain sectors of the event industry, ethics might be seen as an important factor in the planning of events. What sectors might they be, and what specific ethical considerations might they have?

7 Can you think of any leaders in the event industry who could be described as ethical?

8 Read the Leadership in Action section – do you think Mel could be described as an authentic leader? If so, why and if not, why not?

Further reading

Bavik, A. (2020) A systematic review of the servant leadership literature in management and hospitality literature. *International Journal of Contemporary Hospitality Management,* **32**(1), 347-382.

Brown, M.E., Trevion, L.K. & Harrison, D.A. (2005) Ethical leadership: A social learning perspective for construct development and testing. *Organizational Behaviour and Human Decision Processes,* **97**(2) 117-134.

Dhar, R.L. (2016) Ethical leadership and its impact on service innovative behaviour: The role of LMX and job autonomy. *Tourism Management,* **57**, 139-148.

Wang, Z. & Xie, Y. (2019) Authentic leadership and employees' emotional labour in the hospitality industry. *International Journal of Contemporary Hospitality Management,* **32**(2), 797-814.

References

Avolio, B.J., Gardner, W.L., Walumbwa, F.O., Luthans, F. & May, D. R. (2004) Unlocking the mask: a look at the process by which authentic leaders impact follower attitudes and behaviours. *Leadership Quarterly,* **15**(6), 801-823

Avolio, B. J. & Gardner, W. L. (2005). Authentic leadership development – getting to the root of positive forms of leadership. *Leadership Quarterly,* **16**(3), 315-338.

Avolio, B. J., Walumbwa, F. O. & Weber, T. J. (2009). Leadership: current theories, research and future directions. *Annual Review of Psychology,* **60**, 421-429.

Bavik, A. (2020) A systematic review of the servant leadership literature in management and hospitality literature. *International Journal of Contemporary Hospitality Management,* **32**(1), 347-382.

Brown, M.E., Trevion, L.K. & Harrison, D.A. (2005) Ethical leadership: A social learning perspective for construct development and testing. *Organisational Behaviour and Human Decision Processes,* **97**(2), 117-134.

Brownell, J. (2010). Leadership in the service of hospitality. *Cornell Hospitality Quarterly,* **51**(3), 363-378. doi:10.1177/1938965510368651

Dhar, R.L. (2016) Ethical leadership and its impact on service innovative behaviour: The role of LMX and job autonomy. *Tourism Management,* **57**, 139-148

Dinh, J., Lord, R. G., Gardner, W. L., Meuser, J. D., Liden, R. C. & Hu, J. (2014). Leadership theory and research in the new millennium: Current theoretical trends and changing perspectives. *Leadership Quarterly,* **25**(1), 36-62.

Dionne, S., Gupta, A., Sotak, K. L., Shirreffs, K. A., Serban, A., Hao, C., ... Yammarino, F. J. (2014). A 25-year perspective on levels of analysis in leadership research. *Leadership Quarterly,* **25**(1), 6-35.

Eva, N., Robin, M., Sendjaya, S., van Dierendonck, D. & Liden, R. C. (2019). Servant leadership: a systematic review and call for future research. *Leadership Quarterly,* **30**(1), 111-132.

Gardner, W. L., Avolio, B. J., Luthans, F., May, D. R. & Walumbwa, F. O. (2005). Can you see the real me? A self-based model of authentic leader and follower development. *Leadership Quarterly,* **16**(3), 343-372.

Getz, D. & Page, S., (2020). *Event Studies : Theory, Research and Policy for Planned Events* (4th Ed). Abingdon: Routledge.

Greenleaf, R. K. (1977/2002). *Servant-leadership: A journey into the nature of legitimate power and greatness.* Mahwah, NJ: Paulist Press.

Hassan, S., Mahsud, R., Yukl, G. & Prussia, G.E. (2013) Ethical and empowering leadership and leader effectiveness. *Journal of Managerial Psychology,* **28**(2), 133-146.

Hoch, J., Bommer, W., Dulebohn, J. & Dongyuan, W. (2018). Do ethical, authentic and servant leadership explain variance above and beyond transformational leadership? A meta analysis. *Journal of Management,* **44**(2), 501-529.

Huang, J., Li, W., Qiu, C., Yim, H.-k. F. & Wan, J. (2016). The impact of CEO servant leadership on firm performance in the hospitality industry. *International Journal of Contemporary Hospitality Management,* **28**(5), 945-968.

Lemoine, G.J., Hartnell, C.A. & Leroy, H. (2019) Taking stock of moral approaches to leadership: an integrative review of ethical, authentic and servant leadership. *Academy of Management Annals,* **13**(1).

Mayer, D. M., Aquino, K., Greenbaum, R. & Kuenzi, M. (2012). Who displays ethical leadership, and why does it matter? An examination of antecedents and consequences of ethical leadership. *Academy of Management Journal,* **55**(1), 151-171.

Megheirkouni, M. (2018). Insights on practicing of servant leadership in the events sector. *Sport, Business and Management,* **8**(2), 134-152.

Parris, D., & Peachey, J. (2013). Encouraging servant leadership: A qualitative study of how a cause-related sporting event inspires participants to serve. *Leadership,* **9**(4), 486-512.

Spears, L.C. (2010) Character and servant leadership: ten characteristics of effective, caring leaders. The *Journal of Virtues & Leadership,* 1(1), 25-30.

van Dierendonck, D. (2011). Servant Leadership: a review and synthesis. *Journal of Management,* **37**(4), 1228-1261.

Walumbwa, F. O., Avolio, B. J., Gardner, W. L., Wernsing, T. S. & Peterson, S. J. (2008). Authentic leadership: Development and validation of a theory-based measure. *Journal of Management,* **34**, 89-126.

Wang, Z. & Xie, Y. (2019) Authentic leadership and employees' emotional labour in the hospitality industry. *International Journal of Contemporary Hospitality Management.* **32**(2), 797-814.

Wu, L.-Z., Tse, E. C.-Y., Fu, P., Kwan, K. H. & Lui, J. (2013). The impact of servant leadership on hotel employees' servant behaviour. *Cornell Hospitality Quarterly*, **54**(4), 383-395.

Yammarino, F.J. (2013). Leadership – past, present and future. *Journal of Leadership and Organisational Studies*, **20**(1), 149-155.

Yukl, G. Mahsud, R. & Hassan, S. (2013) An improved measure of ethical leadership. *Journal of Leadership & Organisational Studies*. **20**(1) 38-48.

5 Leadership as a collective process

Chapter aims

- ☐ Introduce and critically discuss concepts of collectivistic leadership
- ☐ Explore the differences and similarities in terminology and the problems that creates
- ☐ Critically discuss the use of shared leadership in planned events and event tourism
- ☐ Introduce and critically examine the concept of team leadership
- ☐ Examine the role of social identity theory in leadership
- ☐ Focus on leadership as an enabling action: industry insight from Eamonn Hunt of VeryCreative.

Leadership as a collectivistic process

As we have seen in the previous chapters of this book, one of the criticisms of a large section of leadership studies is that they still mostly focus on the role of those in formal leadership positions. The majority of leadership scholars still tend to study leadership from the perspective of the formal leaders, and with the preconception that leadership stems from a single source. This perspective is referred to as an entity-led perspective – viewing leadership through the lens of the behaviour of one person. By taking this entity-led perspective, leadership studies are still very narrow in focus. However, some scholars have begun to recognise the limitations of 'heroic' or entity-led leadership studies and have instead turned their focus from leadership as something a leader does, towards conceptualising leadership as an influence process (Langley & Tsoukas, 2017; Northouse, 2017).

Some scholars working in this area have developed an understanding that leadership does not necessarily just reside in the nominated 'leader' but in fact may be enacted by multiple individuals, who work in both informal and formal leadership positions. They therefore offer a broad view of leadership, which sees leadership as a process. This means that leadership can be shared, distributed or collectively completed. This new perspective has resulted in yet another significant paradigm shift for leadership studies, which has seen the growth in studies that view leadership as a collectivistic process (Avolio, Walumbwa & Weber, 2009; Badaracco, 2001; Dinh et al., 2014; Gardner et al., 2010).

Various terms have been used to describe these forms of leadership, including collectivistic, shared, distributed, team, dispersed (e.g. Friedrich, Griffith & Mumford, 2016; Pearce, Conger & Locke, 2007; Uhl-Bien, 2006; Yammarino et al., 2012). There are clear differences in most of these terms, but they all share the same emphasis on relationships and on the process of constructing leadership through the collective. The key difference is perhaps described as differing levels of dispersedness (Schedlitzki & Edwards, 2018), each of which will be described in the sections below.

There is, however, conceptual crossover in these perspectives. These can be summarised as:

- They all tend to identify leadership as a social or relational process that emerges from interactions with multiple individuals, and resides in the network of relationships that exist in work groups.

- They recognise leadership wherever it occurs – it is not restricted to a single or small set of leaders but is a dynamic system, in which multiple individuals can carry out leadership activities and functions through collective behaviours, and influence both relationships and social process).

- They largely agree that leadership activities can change over time and that they are also dependent on the larger context in which leadership is embedded.

The rise of collective leadership perspectives

At the core of these new collective leadership perspectives is the view that leadership is a social influence process and as such, organisational teams and individuals are seen as a potential source of leadership, despite having no formal leadership responsibilities. The connection between leadership and teams stems from the changes to the workplace and the increased complexity in the environment in which work is carried out.

For example, some scholars argue that the need to share leadership around an organisation comes from the rapid speed of external changes in technology, operations and strategy that we now see in the workplace. They suggest that organisations must be able to respond quickly to these changes through new job design, increased motivation, management style and rewarded remuneration. In addition, competition has driven organisations to consider new modes of organising and teams have become central to that perspective (Pearce, Manz & Sims, 2009). Organisational structures have therefore evolved to cope with the ambiguity and challenges that change brings, with flatter or networked structures becoming more common (itself a response to the problems with the top-down structures that were common in the past). These flatter structures are useful to organisations because senior leaders may not always have the right information to make decisions and, therefore need to rely on specialised workers who have the knowledge, skills or ability to share the load (Wendt, Euwema & van Emmerik, 2009). However, and given this increased complexity and interconnectedness of work, it has become apparent that individuals are unlikely to have all the skills and behaviours required to effectively perform all the required leadership functions (Northouse, 2017).

In addition, the way in which organisations can now respond to environmental pressures creates a need for changing workplace structures – the speed of which responses are now required, because of the conditions of global integration and competing stakeholder environments (Fitzsimons et al., 2011), means that organisations cannot wait for leadership decisions to be made at the top of the organisation. Instead, the person in charge at any moment is the person with the key knowledge, skills and abilities required for the job in hand – this ensures a faster response to the challenging demands. And of course, the benefits of sharing or distributing leadership around a collective group mean that when there is a change in the required knowledge, skills and abilities, a new expert should step forward to take the lead (Pearce et al., 2009).

Collective, shared or distributed leadership – a note for the reader

Whilst there is a convergence of understanding in these perspectives on leadership, there is also a wide range of diversity and divergence within the conceptualisations – not least in the terms used to describe the range of theories gathered under this label. These types of leadership have been discussed widely in the literature, using a variety of terms including *shared* (e.g. Bergman et al., 2012; Carson et al., 2007; Nicolaides et al., 2014; Pearce & Conger, 2003; Pearce et al., 2007), *distributed* (e.g. Spillane, 2006), *collective* and *collaborative* (e.g. Cullen-Lester & Yammarino, 2016; Friedrich et al., 2016; Friedrich et al., 2009) and *team* leadership (e.g. Day et al., 2004; Ensley et al., 2006; Fitzsimons et al., 2011; Mathieu, et al., 2008). The proliferation of terms used by scholars indicates that there are many strands of theoretical developments related to collectivistic leadership – suggesting that theoretical development in this area is wide and varied. This variety has created uncertainty about whether these terms are all related to the same phenomenon or are unrelated concepts. More often than not, the term collective leadership encompasses shared leadership. Indeed it includes many characteristics of shared leadership, particularly in terms of its emphasis on the relationships that connect the individuals within organisations. In the published research, *shared* leadership tends to dominate, and so, in this book that this the term we shall use.

In another confusing twist, the concepts of shared and distributed leadership are often used interchangeably in scholarly research, which leads to theoretical confusion (for an example of this, see the literature review by Kocolowski, 2010). Whilst many agree that shared and distributed leadership share the same foundations, since the 1990s the theoretical discussions have developed into two distinct conversations, stemming from different areas of research. The extensive work by Fitzsimons et al. (2011, p. 319) highlights the conceptual differences between shared and distributed leadership – they traced the historical origins of shared leadership to organisational management and the team-based literature; and distributed leadership to developments in education.

Echoing this, in a recent systematic literature review, Sweeney, Clarke and Higgs (2019) found that shared leadership was the dominant term used by researchers working within a commercial organisational context, with only one of the 40 studies reviewed using the term distributed leadership. Distributed leadership, on the other hand, is the dominant term used in both education and healthcare research (Bolden, 2011; Sweeney et al., 2019). As this book is specifically about leadership in event management, we focus on shared, not distributed, leadership.

The rest of the chapter describes some of the current collectivistic perspectives on leadership – the reader should be alert to both the clear similarities between concepts and the conceptual divergence.

Shared leadership

The concept of shared leadership is not new – it was first mentioned in the literature in 1948 by Berne and Sheats and in 1954 by Gibb and leadership as a process was being discussed by Brown and Hosking (1986). The most significant contributions to the theoretical development of shared leadership within organisations come from the work of Pearce and colleagues (e.g. Ensley et al., 2006; Pearce & Conger, 2003; Pearce & Manz, 2005; Pearce et al., 2004; Wassenaar & Pearce, 2012; Zhang et al., 2014). Their work stemmed from an acceptance that leadership does not solely reside in one single person, and that with an increase in teamwork in organisations, it is more likely that multiple team members will engage with leadership functions. Theories around shared leadership therefore focus on whether and to what end team members share leadership of the team.

Whilst there are some variants in the definitions of shared leadership in the scholarly literature, what is notable is that they articulate consistent themes, viewing leadership as an emergent process of influencing organisational peers, clearly distinct from the traditional forms of hierarchical leadership (Pearce et al., 2009; Sweeney et al., 2019). In an analysis of shared leadership research, Zhu et al. (2018, p. 837) noted that across the different conceptualisations, there are three key common characteristics – a brief summation of this discussion is given below.

1 Shared leadership is about horizontal, lateral influence among peers. In work teams, there are two sources of leadership – vertical, hierar-

chical leadership from the formal leader and leadership that stems from team members. Shared leadership focuses on the latter, but it should be noted that scholars do not suggest that the two sources of leadership are mutually exclusive. In fact, shared leadership scholars agree (and have empirically demonstrated) that both sources of leadership are important.

2   Shared leadership is a team phenomenon. In contrast to traditional views of leadership as a phenomenon that derives from a single individual, shared leadership highlights leadership as an emergent property of a collective. Leadership influence is shared among members at group level.

3   Leadership roles and influence are dispersed across team members. Whereas entity-led views of leadership regard leadership as centralised around one leader, shared leadership suggests leadership is broadly distributed across team members.

There is an agreement then among the conceptualisations of shared leadership that there is little support for single individuals having a dramatic impact on organisational performance. Scholars argue instead that leadership can be shared away from the top of the organisation, and that people engage in leadership practices at many levels, in both informal and formal roles (Clarke, 2012; Currie & Lockett, 2011). Concepts of shared leadership therefore focus on the broad sharing of power and influence among multiple team members, who can apply influence over each other in order to engage in leadership that will enhance performance of teams and organisations. Shared leadership differs from other forms of collective leadership in that they describe a set of cooperatively orientation attitudes, thoughts and actions through which team members convert member inputs to member outputs (Wang et al., 2014).

Pearce and colleagues were among the first to advance shared leadership theory within team based research, and it is their conceptualisation that is most often cited in literature (e.g. Dinh et al., 2014; Ensley et al., 2006; Fausing et al., 2015; Hoch, 2013, 2014; Hoch & Dulebohn, 2013; Kozlowski, 2016; Serban & Roberts, 2016; Sweeney et al., 2019; Wu & Cormican, 2016). Shared leadership is defined as *"A dynamic, interactive influence process among individuals and groups for which the objective is to lead one another to the achievement of group or organizational goals or both"* (pg. 1). As such, shared leadership is a simultaneous, ongoing, mutual influence process in which individual team members share in behaviours and roles of the traditional leader in order to maximize the performance of the team (Pearce, 2004; Pearce & Conger, 2003).

There are, of course, criticisms of shared leadership, not least around the core question of who leads, and when. Scholars who have tackled this try to draw distinctions between the misconception that shared leadership means that everyone leads all the time and the real meaning of shared leadership, which is that everyone has the opportunity to lead, if they are willing and the resources and freedom are available to them. Carson et al.'s (2007) conceptualisation also recognises the temporal nature of shared leadership, and suggests that it can be placed on a continuum based on the number of leadership sources having a high degree of influence on the team.

There is a growing body of evidence that indicates that there is a positive relationship between team effectiveness and performance and shared leadership (for meta-analyses, see Nicolaides et al., 2014; Wang et al., 2014). When team members commit to sharing their leadership with their team members in order to achieve the organisation's or team's missions and goals, they commit to using more of their personal resources, sharing more information and engaging with the complex tasks at a higher level (Avolio et al., 2009; Pearce & Sims, 2002). These commitments from team members allow the team effectiveness and performance to improve (Evaggelia & Vitta, 2012; Fitzsimons et al., 2011).

Other outcome related research found that shared leadership created an increase in innovative behaviour (D'Innocenzo et al., 2016; Ensley et al., 2006; Hoch, 2014; Nicolaides et al., 2014; Pearce & Sims, 2002; Serban & Roberts, 2016) and team satisfaction (Mehra et al., 2006). Researchers have also found that teams with shared leadership experience less conflict, greater consensus and higher trust and cohesion than teams without shared leadership (Bergman et al., 2012; Fransen et al., 2015). There is a significant amount of research that confirms that high levels of shared leadership can promote team effectiveness by providing teams with intangible, relational resources that facilitate sharing information, expressing diverse opinions and co-ordinating member actions in the face of uncertain and ambiguous situations. In short, and given these underpinning factors, where multiple team members participate in the sharing of leadership, performace improves (Carson et al., 2007).

Scott-Young, Georgy and Grisinger (2019) conducted a systematic literature review from multiple disciplines in order to introduce shared leadership into the project management domain – clearly useful for those of us interested in planned events. The paper offers a very detailed and comprehensive review of the extant literature which suggests that shared leadership is

"...a construct that may add value to project management practice. Shared leadership has the potential to enhance both project team functioning and project performance, as well as to contribute positively to both individual and wider organisational outcomes."
(Scott-Young et al., 2019, p. 578)

The authors conclude that *"The practice of shared leadership broadens the options for leading project teams, especially in complex, innovative, or knowledge-intensive projects, beyond the traditional practice of a single project manager exercising formal vertical power over team followers."* (Scott-Young et al., 2019, p. 578). Here then, we can see a clear argument forming for the relevance of shared leadership to a planned event context, given the interdependent nature of teams within event organisations, the time-bound and pressurised nature of delivering experiences and the creative output of organisations themselves.

Benson and Blackman (2011) and Hristov and Zehrer (2019) focused on whether the related concept of distributed leadership was beneficial to introduce to destination management organisations. Both studies concluded that tourism organisations might find the adoption of distributed leadership advantageous to increase organisational performance.

Team leadership

Team leadership is a broader construct than other forms of collectivistic leadership. It is fundamentally orientated around enhancing team performance and the satisfaction of the team needs. As Morgeson, Derue and Karam (2010a) suggest, *"team leadership can thus be viewed as oriented around team need satisfaction (with the ultimate aim of fostering team effectiveness). Whoever (inside or outside the team) assumes responsibility for satisfying a team's needs can be viewed as taking on a team leadership role."* (pg.7). Many view other conceptualisations, such as shared or collective leadership, as forms of team leadership (Zhu et al., 2018).

Many teams still have individuals who are primarily responsible for achieving team goals and these formal leadership positions and their effect on team performance is the area that much of the extant research on leadership in teams focuses on, with research indicating that leaders are one of the critical factors in team performance (see the meta-analysis by Burke et al., 2006 for a review of these studies). Some scholars go further – suggesting that leaders are the key factor for success in teams (Nicolaides et al., 2014) and others suggest that team leaders are the reason for failures in organisational teams (Nielsen, 2004). The traditional research into team leadership theories then concentrated on how leaders create and manage effective teams – leadership is viewed as an input to team processes and performance (Day et al., 2004). Team leadership theories therefore take a functional approach, in which they consider that the leaders' effectiveness is based on their ability to ensure that all functions that are critical to the task and team are completed (Burke et al., 2006). Under this approach, leadership is not necessarily undertaken by one person (i.e. it can be distributed among a team), but the leader is responsible for ensuring that the functions are accomplished. In other words, formal team leaders are still important here – when a leadership activity requires different capabilities, the best team leaders will ask other team members to assist, ensuring that team leadership is a team activity.

Some scholars have used the term 'team leadership' to suggest that anyone who is able to identify and fulfil a critical function at the right moment is exhibiting team leadership (Zaccaro et al., 2001) – this, we can see, is the same as some conceptualisations of shared leadership. And so here I agree with Day et al. (2006) who state that it is important to distinguish between leaders of teams and their impact on team processes and outcomes, and leadership that develops within a team and the effects that it has. Furthermore, in studying the shared aspects of leadership, it is important for scholars to distinguish the level at which leadership is conceptualised. This, of course, echoes the criticisms of conceptualising leadership at the individual or dyadic level.

Taking this argument further, Morgeson, DeRue and Karam (2010b) suggest there are three reasons why the body of work that focuses on team leadership may not add value to an understanding of leadership.

First, they state, team leadership research has focused on a narrow set of leadership activities, which has resulted in a limited understanding of the range of ways leaders can help teams to succeed. Second, there is a gap in our understanding of the interchange between leadership processes and teams. Last, they suggest that research to date has focused on formal team leadership structures and has failed to recognise the 'long-recognised' fact that leadership is distributed within a team. They stress the importance of the need to understand the role of leadership in the context of the team and the difference leadership sources that exist – without this, scholars risk providing an incomplete account of the ways in which leadership can help teams to success. They suggest there are four sources of leadership, which they categorise as being located internally (to the team) and externally (of the team) and which can be either formal or informal (see Table 5.1)

	Formal	Informal
Internal	Team leader Project manager	Shared Emergent
External	Sponsor Coach Team advisor	Mentor Champion Executive coordinator

Table 5.1: Sources of leadership in teams from Morgeson et al. (2010a)

Social identity theories of leadership

Some theorists have noted that, in order for teams to function, they must share an identity, which is created through the exchanges that take place within the group (Reicher, Haslam & Platow, 2018). Here, scholars are drawing from concepts of social identity in social psychology applied to teamwork – these theories suggest that individuals build their concept of their self through the social groups that exist at work and these identities influence our ability to work with others. When people share a common sense of social identity, their behaviour is underpinned by a sense of connection which is drawn from common norms, values, beliefs and goals (Reicher et al., 2018) and this aids them to agree on issues impacting on the group, via consensus. Further, shared identity creates feelings of unification as team members share an investment in the work that they do, which results in an enhanced sense of trust. These feelings of connectivity, unification and trust are some of the ways in which a shared social identity helps to improve the way teams perform in an organisation. Social identity in teams can therefore be simplified to defining 'who we are' and 'what we do' and it follows that if individuals are able to shape the shared social identity, then they are in a position to influence the actions of the team members (Hogg et al., 2012).

Whilst some social identity theorists have focused on those in formal leadership positions, others have focused on whether leaders are emerging from, or being selected by, the team because of their prototypicality to the rest of the team. Here, the emergence of a leader is based on a group member's resemblance to a prototypical leader as determined by other group members. The most prototypical member of the group becomes the leader through social categorisation and, because of this, has the appearance of having the most influence – this influence becomes reality through "...*social attraction processes that make followers agree and comply with leader's ideas and suggestions*" (Hogg, 2001, p. 184). Social identity theory of leadership then centres on the need for people to identify strongly with a group, and as that group becomes more influenced by prototypicality, the member that most represents the typical qualities begins to emerge as leader. Leaders are considered effective because they embody and influence the relationships that form part of the shared identity and leaders who don't pay attention to the social identity within the team are less likely to be accepted than those that do.

These identity-based approaches to leadership have been examined in a number of studies (e.g. Fielding & Hogg, 1997; Hogg, 2001, 2010; Hogg, Hains & Mason, 1998; Hogg et al., 2012; Uhl-Bien et al., 2014; van Knippenberg, 2012; Van Vugt & De Cremer, 1999) – these studies suggest that group prototypicality and social attraction are at least as important as leadership characteristics. The prototypicality of the leader therefore has a key influencing factor on the effectiveness of leadership. The leader's role is therefore about shaping social identities so that the leader's proposals are seen as a manifestation of the team's beliefs and values (Haslam, Reicher & Platow, 2011). The leader's role is related to the team they lead thus:

♦ Being one of us – enacting 'us;'

♦ Doing it for us – acting and modelling fairness and group interest;

- ◆ Crafting a sense of us – being entrepreneurs of identity;
- ◆ Making us matter – identity management, purpose and power in the wider context.

Steffens et al., (2014)

More recently, research has noted that whilst the notion of prototypicality (being 'one of us' and understanding the team's social identity) is an important element in leadership, it is not the only factor that matters. Reicher et al. (2018) note two further things are needed – the first is that leaders need to prioritise working for the in-group above their own personal interests, or the interests of the out-group. The second is that the leader's actions must contribute to achievement of the team goals and be aligned with the values and priorities that have been defined by the shared team identity. These two further considerations are significant to social identity theories of leadership as they help to solve the inherent tensions that happen because shared identity increases followership and enhances the position of the leader. It is easy then for the leader to get the credit and reward for the team's success – and if the leader isn't perceived to be working hard to understand and meet the needs of the team, then the perception of the leader 'being one of us' is undermined and the social identity among the team reduces.

Summary

This chapter has sought to clarify the workplace conditions that have resulted in organisations moving towards different types of leadership. It has drawn the reader's attention to the development of collective theories of leadership which have emerged as potential solutions to the current challenges in the workplace. This departure from viewing leadership as something an individual does is seen by some as radical in terms of leadership studies – certainly it requires a change in mindset from the leadership described in previous chapters. In these collective forms of leadership, where leadership is thought of as emerging from group relationships, it is more important to understand the nature of both the network and the relationships within it, than to look at how those in formal leadership positions lead, and what effects they might have. The types of leadership described in this chapter can be summarised as:

- **Shared leadership** is described by Pearce (2004, p. 48) as a *"... simultaneous, on-going, mutual influence process within a team that is characterized by serial emergence of official and unofficial leaders."*

- The term shared leadership was developed from **'team-based' leadership** literature and is widely used in the management/ organisational studies research fields.

- **Team leadership** is a broader construct than other forms of collectivistic leadership. It is fundamentally orientated around enhancing team performance and the satisfaction of the team needs.

- **Social identity in leadership** suggest that, in order for teams to function, they must share an identity, which is created through the exchanges that take place within the group.

Leadership in action: Industry insight from Eamonn Hunt, VeryCreative

Eamonn has been around the events industry since the late 1970's. Whilst at school Eamonn hired the school hall and started promoting his own concerts, he also started his own record duplication business to sell live recordings of the bands that he was involved with. Eamonn later joined Sheffield Theatres where he cut his teeth as a theatre lighting designer. In 1982 he went to the Edinburgh festival for the first time as assistant designer for Hull Truck Theatre Company and met other theatre companies and bands that went on to use his design and production services. Eamonn built a reputation for creating visually exciting 'theatrical' concert lighting, which in turn led to experimenting with large scale projection and animation, leading to him working on many of the major tours and large scale commercial events of the eighties and nineties, including the Olympic Games and Millennium Celebrations.

Eventually Eamonn decided to set up his own company offering design and project management to show producers, which in turn led to the creation of VeryCreative and subsequent companies that each offer some form of specialised live event support service. VeryCreative specialise in event conceptualisation, innovative design and event production for the

5: Leadership as a collective process

industry. In a nutshell, VeryCreative are creative ideas people. They take clients' problems and provide innovative event solutions. VeryCreative work in theatre, television, live concert touring, exhibitions, product launches, brand activations, and web based blended events.

Leadership is not about being the big boss; it is about accepting the responsibility to deliver a project, whether that be for a client or inhouse, and to build and nurture a team to deliver that project. Mine is an enabling role; to look at the bigger picture and help the team to navigate the right path to our objective whilst providing a safe environment where everyone on the team can excel and reach their full potential. My team need to understand that I will provide a safety net of support to help them; that I will guide them and encourage them, and that I will help them reflect on their crises and their achievements, but that I will also be critical and if necessary intervene to prevent them from damaging the team, they need to know that everyone is accountable for reaching our full potential and our goal, and that everyone will be equally rewarded for achieving success, whether that be delivering an exceptional event for a client or simple ensuring that we have the right systems in place to provide cover for each other if we are sick.

For me leadership is not just about being a manager, it is about being a reference point and an enabler, allowing others to manage themselves. I have to be incredibly aware of my own attitude to change and the constantly evolving environment that I work in. I must be insightful and agile, forever monitoring the ways that other organisations and teams are evolving their practices and their outputs. It is essential for me to reflect often on what has been achieved within my team and what we are aiming to achieve, and it is down to me, in consultation with my team to effect change in a meaningful way. Never has this been more necessary than in the COVID pandemic that swept the world in 2020.

With live events prohibited, the need to change our offer rapidly and successfully was immediate, but even more pressing was the need to support my team in a rapidly evolving moment of crisis. Acutely conscious that the team were looking to me for leadership, my first priority was to protect them from their own doubts and fears, they needed to know that their jobs were secure, that their income was protected and that they would be supported in whatever way I and the company were able, no matter if that was job related or personal. The manner in which I lead would have to change, I would need to focus more on personal individualised support and less on production outputs, I would have to help each person visualise what the new event landscape will look like whilst simultaneously building what may only be temporary measures; an online platform for events and a protocol and delivery mechanism for socially distanced live events. All whilst they and I would have to deal with the extra burden of home schooling, family bereavement and financial insecurity brought about by the COVID pandemic.

Needless to say that while circumstances change, leadership in any situation is fundamentally the same; build trust, respect one another, have clear objectives, prepare for success, support each other in setbacks, celebrate achievements together.

Study questions

1 Do you think these ideas of collectivistic leadership are unrealistic? Discuss if leadership as a collective activity could really work in an event organisation.

2 Planned events need one 'heroic' leader, in a formal leadership position who takes responsibility for all decisions, and is in control of the event plan. Critically examine this statement.

3 How do the various notions of collectivistic leadership compare and contrast with each other?

4 Where have you experienced shared leadership? What were the positive and negative aspects of it, and why?

5 Clarke (2012) suggests that shared leadership would be very useful for project management. Describe the stages in the event project cycle when you think shared leadership might work better than traditional hierarchical leadership.

6 Discuss how the concept of team leadership might enhance the planning of an event.

7 Think about a team you are part of. Do you think you share any kind of identity? List the things you have in common.

8 In the Leadership in action section, Eamonn found himself moving towards a more collectivistic approach to leadership. Describe the reasons for this, and the benefits of this approach in that situation.

Further reading

Badaracco, J. (2001). We don't need another hero. *Harvard Business Review,* **79**(8), 120-126.

Carson, J., Tesluk, P. E. & Marrone, J. A. (2007). Shared leadership in teams: An investigation of antecedent conditions and performance. *Academy of Management Journal,* **50**(5), 1217-1234.

Clarke, N. (2012). Leadership in projects: what we know from the literature and new insights. *Team Performance Management: An International Journal,* 18(3-4), 128-148. doi:10.1108/13527591211241042.

Pearce, C. L. & Conger, J. (2003). *Shared Leadership: Reframing the hows and whys of leadership.* Thousand Oaks, CA: Sage.

van Knippenberg, D. (2012). Leadership and Identity. In D. V. Day & J. Antonakis (Eds.), *The Nature of Leadership* (2nd ed., pp. 477-507). Thousand Oaks, CA: Sage.

References

Avolio, B. J., Walumbwa, F. O. & Weber, T. J. (2009). Leadership: current theories, research and future directions. *Annual Review of Psychology,* **60**, 421-429.

Badaracco, J. (2001). We don't need another hero. *Harvard Business Review,* **79**(8), 120-126.

Benson, A. M. & Blackman, D. (2011). To distribute leadership or not? A lesson from the islands. *Tourism Management,* **32**(5), 1141-1149.

Bergman, J.Z., Rentsch, J.R., Small, E.E., Davenport, S.W. & Bergman, S.M. (2012) The shared leadership process in decision-making teams. *Journal of Social Psychology,* **152**(1), 17-42. doi:10.1080/00224545.2010.538763.

Bolden, R. (2011). Distributed leadership in organizations: a review of theory and research. *International Journal of Management Reviews,* **13**(3), 251-269.

Brown, M. H. & Hosking, D. M. (1986). Distributed leadership and skilled perfomance as successful organisation in social movements. *Human Relations,* **39**(1), 65-79.

Burke, C. S., Stagl, K. C., Klein, C., Goodwin, G. F., Salas, E. & Halpin, S. M. (2006). What type of leadership behaviors are functional in teams? A meta-analysis. *Leadership Quarterly,* **17**(3), 288-307. doi:10.1016/j.leaqua.2006.02.007.

Carson, J., Tesluk, P. E. & Marrone, J. A. (2007). Shared leadership in teams: An investigation of antecedent conditions and performance. *Academy of Management Journal,* **50**(5), 1217-1234.

Clarke, N. (2012). Leadership in projects: what we know from the literature and new insights. *Team Performance Management,* **18**(3-4), 128-148. doi:10.1108/13527591211241042.

Cullen-Lester, K. L. & Yammarino, F. J. (2016). Collective and network approaches to leadership: Special issue introduction. *Leadership Quarterly,* **27**(2), 173-180. doi:10.1016/j.leaqua.2016.02.001.

Currie, G. & Lockett, A. (2011). Distributing leadership in health and social care: concertive, conjoint or collective? *International Journal of Management Reviews,* **13**(3), 286-300.

D'Innocenzo, L., Mathieu, J. E. & Kukenberger, M. R. (2016). A meta-analysis of different forms of shared leadership–team performance relations. *Journal of Management,* **42**(7), 1964-1991. doi:10.1177/0149206314525205.

Day, D. V., Gronn, P. & Salas, E. (2004). Leadership capacity in teams. *The Leadership Quarterly,* **15**(6), 857-880. doi:10.1016/j.leaqua.2004.09.001.

Day, D. V., Gronn, P. & Salas, E. (2006). Leadership in team-based organizations: On the threshold of a new era. *Leadership Quarterly,* **17**(3), 211-216.

Dinh, J., Lord, R. G., Gardner, W. L., Meuser, J. D., Liden, R. C. & Hu, J. (2014). Leadership theory and research in the new millennium: Current theoretical trends and changing perspectives. *Leadership Quarterly,* **25**(1), 36-62.

Ensley, M. D., Hmieleski, K. M. & Pearce, C. L. (2006). The importance of vertical and shared leadership within new venture top management teams: Implications for the performance of startups. *Leadership Quarterly,* **17**(3), 217-231. doi:10.1016/j.leaqua.2006.02.002.

Evaggelia, F. & Vitta, A. (2012). Is shared leadership the new way of management? Comparision between vertical and shared leadership. *Science Journal of Business Management*, **2012**(2), 5.

Fausing, M. S., Joensson, T. S., Lewandowski, J. & Bligh, M. (2015). Antecedents of shared leadership: empowering leadership and interdependence. *Leadership & Organization Development Journal*, **36**(3), 271-291. doi:10.1108/LODJ-06-2013-0075.

Fielding, K. S. & Hogg, M. A. (1997). Social identity, self-categorization, and leadership: a field study of small interactive groups. *Group Dynamics: Theory, Research, and Practice*, **1**(1), 39-51. doi:10.1037/1089-2699.1.1.39.

Fitzsimons, D., James, K. T. & Denyer, D. (2011). Alternative approaches for studying shared and distributed leadership. *International Journal of Management Reviews*, **13**(3), 313.

Fransen, K., Van Puyenbroeck, S., Loughead, T. M., Vanbeselaere, N., De Cuyper, B., Vande Broek, G. & Boen, F. (2015). Who takes the lead? Social network analysis as a pioneering tool to investigate shared leadership within sports teams. *Social Networks*, **43**, 28-38. doi:10.1016/j.socnet.2015.04.003.

Friedrich, T., Griffith, J. & Mumford, M. (2016). Collective leadership behaviours: evaluating the leader, team network and problem situation characteristics that influence their use. *Leadership Quarterly*, **27**(2), 312-333.

Friedrich, T., Vessey, W.B., Schuelke, M.J., Mumford, M., Yammarino, F.J. & Ruark, G.A. (2009). A framework for understanding collective leadership: the selective utlisation of leader and team expertise within networks. *Leadership Quarterly*, **20**(6), 933-958.

Gardner, W.L., Lowe, K.B., Moss, T.W., Mahoney, K.T. & Cogliser, C.C. (2010). Scholarly leadership of the study of leadership: a review of *The Leadership Quarterly's* second decade, 2000-2009. *Leadership Quarterly*, **21**(6), 922-958.

Haslam, A., Reicher, S. D., & Platow, M. J. (2011). *The New Psychology of Leadership:Identity, influence and power*. New York: Psychology Press.

Hoch, J. (2013). Shared leadership and innovation: the role of vertical leadership and employee integrity. *Journal of Business and Psychology*, **28**(2), 159-174. doi:10.1007/s10869-012-9273-6.

Hoch, J. (2014). Shared leadership, diversity, and information sharing in teams. *Journal of Managerial Psychology*, **29**(5), 541-564. doi:10.1108/JMP-02-2012-0053.

Hoch, J. & Dulebohn, J. (2013). Shared leadership in enterprise resource planning and human resource management system implementation. *Human Resource Management Review, 23*(1), 114-125. doi:10.1016/j. hrmr.2012.06.007.

Hogg, M. A. (2001). A social identity theory of leadership. *Personality and Social Psychology Review, 5*(3), 184-200. doi:10.1207/S15327957PSPR0503_1.

Hogg, M. A. (2010). Influence and leadership. In S. T. Fiske, D. T. Gilbert & G. Lindzey (Eds.), *Handbook of Social Psychology* (5th ed., pp. 1166-1207). New York: John Wiley & Sons.

Hogg, M. A., Hains, S. C. & Mason, I. (1998). Identification and leadership in small groups: salience, frame of reference, and leader stereotypicality effects on leader evaluations. *Journal of Personality and Social Psychology, 75*(5), 1248-1263. doi:10.1037/0022-3514.75.5.1248.

Hogg, M. A., Van Knippenberg, D. & Rast, D. (2012). The social identity theory of leadership: theoretical origins, research findings, and conceptual developments. *European Review of Social Psychology, 23*(1), 258-304doi:10.1080/10463283.2012.741134.

Hristov, D. & Zehrer, A. (2019). Does distributed leadership have a place in destination managment organisations? A policy makers perspective. *Current Issues in Tourism, 22*(9), 1095-1115.

Kocolowski, M. (2010). Shared leadership: is it time for a change? *Emerging Leadership Journeys, 3*(1), 22-32.

Kozlowski, S. (2016). Team-centric leadership: An integrative review. *Annual Review of Organisational Psychology and Organisational Behaviour, 3*, 21-54.

Langley, A. & Tsoukas, H. (Eds.). (2017). *The SAGE Handbook of Process Organisation Studies*. London: Sage.

Mathieu, J. E., Maynard, M. T., Rapp, T. & Gilson, L. L. (2008). Team effectiveness 1997-2007: a review of recent advancements and a glimpse into the future. *Journal of Management, 34*(3), 410-476.

Mehra, A., Smith, B. R., Dixon, A. L. & Robertson, B. (2006). Distributed leadership in teams: the network of leadership perceptions and team performance. *Leadership Quarterly, 17*(3), 232-245. doi:10.1016/j. leaqua.2006.02.003.

Morgeson, F., Derue, D. S. & Karam, E. P. (2010a). Leadership in teams - a functional approach to understanding leadership structures and proesses. *Journal of Management, 36*(1), 5-39.

Morgeson, F., DeRue, D. S. & Karam, E. P. (2010b). Leadership in teams: a functional approach to understanding leadership structures and processes. *Journal of Management*, **36**(1), 5-39. doi:10.1177/0149206309347376.

Nicolaides, V. C., Laport, K. A., Chen, T. R., Tomassetti, A. J., Weis, E. J., Zaccaro, S. J. & Cortina, J. M. (2014). The shared leadership of teams: A meta-analysis of proximal, distal, and moderating relationships. *Leadership Quarterly*, **25**(5), 923-942.

Nielsen, J. S. (2004). *The Myth of Leadership: Creating leaderless organisations*. New York: Davies-Black Publishing.

Northouse, P. (2017). *Introduction to Leadership: Concepts and practice*. Thousand Oaks, CA: Sage.

Pearce, C. L. (2004). The future of leadership: combining vertical and shared leadership to transform knowledge work. *Academy of Management Executive*, **18**(1), 47-59. doi:10.5465/AME.2004.12690298.

Pearce, C. L. & Conger, J. (2003). *Shared Leadership: Reframing the hows and whys of leadership*. Thousand Oaks, CA: Sage.

Pearce, C. L., Conger, J. & Locke, E. A. (2007). Shared leadership theory. *The Leadership Quarterly*, **18**(3), 281-288.

Pearce, C. L. & Manz, C. (2005). The new silver bullets of leadership: the importance of self and shared leadership in knowledge work. *Management Department Faculty Publications, 72*.

Pearce, C. L., Manz, C. & Sims, H. P. (2009). Where do we go from here? Is shared leadership the key to team success. *Organisational Dynamics*, **38**(3), 234-238.

Pearce, C. L. & Sims, H. P. (2002). Vertical versus shared leadership as predictors of the effectiveness of change management teams: an examination of aversive, directive, transactional, transformational, and empowering leader behaviors. *Group Dynamics: Theory, Research, and Practice*, **6**(2), 172-197. doi:10.1037/10892699.6.2.172.

Pearce, C. L., Yoo, Y. & Alavi, M. (2004). Leadership, social work and virtual teams: The relative influence of vertical versus shared leadership in the nonprofit sector. In R. Riggio, S. Smith-Orr, & J. Shakely (Eds.), *Improving Leadership in Nonprofit Organsiations* (pp. 180-204). San Fransicso: Jossey-Bass.

Reicher, S. D., Haslam, A. & Platow, M. J. (2018). Shared social identity in leadership. *Current Opinion in Psychology*, **23**, 129-133.

Schedlitzki, D., & Edwards, G. (2018). *Studying leadership: traditonal and critical approaches* (2nd ed.). London: Sage.

Scott-Young, C. M., Georgy, M. & Grisinger, A. (2019). Shared leadership in project teams: An integrative multi-level conceptual model and research agenda. *International Journal Of Project Management,* **37**, 565-581.

Serban, A. & Roberts, A. J. B. (2016). Exploring antecedents and outcomes of shared leadership in a creative context: A mixed-methods approach. *The Leadership Quarterly,* **27**(2), 181-199. doi:10.1016/j.leaqua.2016.01.009.

Spillane, J. P. (2006). *Distributed Leadership.* San Francisco: Josey-Bass, Wiley.

Steffens, N. K., Haslam, A., Reicher, S. D., Platow, M. J., Fransen, K., Yang, J., ... Boen, F. (2014). Leadership as social identity management: introducing the Identity Leadership Inventory (ILI) to assess and validate a four-dimensional model. *Leadership Quarterly,* **25**(5), 1001-1024. doi:10.1016/j.leaqua.2014.05.002.

Sweeney, A., Clarke, N. & Higgs, M. (2019). Shared leadership in commercial organisations: A systematic review of definitions, theoretical frameworks and organisational outcomes. *International Journal of Management Reviews,* **21**(1), 115-136.

Uhl-Bien, M. (2006). Relational Leadership Theory: exploring the social processes of leadership and organizing. *Leadership Quarterly,* **17**(6), 654-676.

Uhl-Bien, M., Riggio, R., Lowe, K. B. & Carsten, M. K. (2014). Followership Theory: a review and research agenda. *Leadership Quarterly,* **25**(1), 83-104.

van Knippenberg, D. (2012). Leadership and identity. In D. V. Day & J. Antonakis (Eds.), *The Nature of Leadership* (2nd ed., pp. 477-507). Thousand Oaks, CA: Sage.

Van Vugt, M. & De Cremer, D. (1999). Leadership in social dilemmas: The effects of group identification on collective actions to provide public goods. *Journal of Personality and Social Psychology,* **76**(4), 587-599. doi:10.1037/0022-3514.76.4.587.

Wang, D., Waldman, D. A. & Zhang, Z. (2014). A meta-analysis of shared leadership and team effectiveness. *Journal of Applied Psychology,* **99**(2), 181-198.

Wassenaar, C. L. & Pearce, C. L. (2012). The nature of shared leadership. In D. V. Day & J. Antonakis (Eds.), *The Nature of Leadership* (2nd ed.). Thousand Oaks: Sage.

Wendt, K. E., Euwema, M. C. & van Emmerik, I. J. H. (2009). Leadership and team cohesiveness across cultures. *Leadership Quarterly,* **20**(3), 358-370.

Wu, Q., & Cormican, K. (2016). Shared ladership and team creativity: a social network analysis in engineering design teams. *Journal of Technology Management and Innovation,* **11**(2), 2-12.

Yammarino, F. J., Salas, E., Serban, A. & Shirreffs, K. A. (2012). Collectivist leadership approaches: putting the 'we' in leadership science and practice. *Industrial and Organisational Psychology,* **5**, 382-402.

Zaccaro, S. J., Rittman, A. L. & Marks, M. A. (2001). Team leadership. *The Leadership Quarterly,* **12**(4), 451-483. doi:10.1016/S1048-9843(01)00093-5.

Zhang, W., Wang, H. & Pearce, C. L. (2014). Consideration for future consequences as an antecedent of transformational leadership behavior: The moderating effects of perceived dynamic work environment. *Leadership Quarterly,* **25**(2), 329-343.

Zhu, J., Liao, Z., Chi Yam, K. & Johnson, R. (2018). Shared leadership: a state of the art review and future research agenda. *Journal of Organisational Behaviour,* **39**(7), 834-852.

6 Leadership as a skill

Chapter aims

- ☐ Introduces the concept of leadership as a skill
- ☐ Explore Mumford's approach to leadership skills
- ☐ Understand the difference between a skill and a competency
- ☐ Critically examine competency theory
- ☐ Understand the variety of competencies that have been identified as important to event leadership
- ☐ Focus on leadership in action: the skills you need to be a successful event manager, by David Strafford of Hopper Events.

Leadership as a skill

In both the event industry, and in scholarly research, leadership is often considered as a skill. This school of thought is closely related to the trait theories of leadership, as conceptually, it is hard to differentiate between the personality traits leaders possess and the skills that they demonstrate. What is the difference between the terms? Well, it is widely accepted that traits are innate, but skills can be learnt (Athey & Orth, 1999). So, skills differ from traits because they are considered to be something that can be developed – a practised ability. A skill is the ability to do a job well, particularly if you have practiced it. This school of thought therefore suggests that you might not be a 'natural leader', but you can develop the necessary set of skills that will allow you to become a good one. As such, you can develop the capabilities required to lead (Mumford et al., 2000b).

This area of leadership study suggests that leadership depends on an 'interactive package of complex skills' (Mumford et al., 2000a, p. 156). Mumford and his colleagues (2000a) present a skills-based model of leadership performance, which suggests that the performance of a leader is based on three key types of skills:

1 Complex problem-solving skills

2 Solution construction skills

3 Social judgement skills

In other words, effective leaders must define problems, gather information, formulate ideas and construct a plan to solve a problem. They must then ensure that others are willing to work towards these solutions with them, which requires social skills such as persuasion, negotiation, judgement and decision-making. Mumford et al. (2000a) suggest that, in order to be an effective leader, individuals must also have a body of knowledge or expertise.

Whilst there was a lot of interest in leadership skills at the turn of the century, this focus is now thought to be too simplistic. The criticism here is similar to those arguments about the inadequacy of the trait theories (see Chapter 2) - namely that reducing leadership to a list of measurable skills ignores the myriad of other inputs to leadership, such as behaviours, context or the followers themselves. However, scholars have not completely rejected the idea that there might exist a set of capabilities that result in effective leadership. Instead, they take a broader view, moving from the term *leadership skills* to *leadership competencies*.

The terms skills and competences are often used interchangeably, but they are not the same. A skill is a specific ability, normally related to certain tasks, whereas a competency tends to incorporate more than just a set of skills – if applied correctly, the term should also acknowledge knowledge, behaviours and traits or abilities. These competency-based theories of leadership therefore recognise that people can learn different sorts of leadership competencies in order to lead in different styles.

Competency based leadership

The earliest work on competencies was by McClelland (1973), who viewed them in a very broad way, as a behavioural attribute that contributed to success. This view of what people do in order to be successful led to the development of competency profiling. Here competencies are defined as skills, motives, traits, abilities or personal characteristics that lead to effective job performance in leadership or managerial occupations (Boyatzis, 1982, 2009; Koenigsfeld et al., 2011; Sandwith, 1993). These competencies can be technical, intellectual or emotional in nature.

- **Technical** – or managerial – competencies can be described as an understanding of, and proficiency in, a specific kind of activity (Schedlitzki & Edwards, 2018).

- **Intellectual** competencies are the cognitive abilities of an individual – their IQ and their ability to use the knowledge or insight from their own intelligence.

- **Emotional** competencies are defined as the leader's emotional intelligence – the ability to define and manage your own emotions, and those of the people around you. Emotionally intelligent people use the emotional information they gather to guide their own behaviours.

Scholars researching competencies in leadership are therefore concerned with identifying the specific competencies within each of these three areas that contribute to the development of successful leaders.

Competency views of leadership can, in many ways, be seen as little more than an extension of the trait theories of leadership (Clarke, 2012) – scholars are still often only concerned with what skills the individual leader possesses, and competency theories of leaderships often result in a list of skills that detail the knowledge that people need in order to successfully do their jobs (e.g. Dulewicz & Higgs, 2005; Koenigsfeld et al., 2011; MBECS, 2011; Müller & Turner, 2010; Sandwith, 1993). This focus on producing a list of skills for successful leadership is actually very useful for the event industry, as it gives those responsible for recruitment and training something specific to work towards. In recent years, the rapid change to the global environment have resulted in changes to the strategic focus of the event industry, and one of the key issues is that of the fast turnover of staff, which creates both strategic and operational human resource management issues for event organisations. To meet these challenges, and to overcome the related challenges in recruitment and retention, much academic research in events, tourism and hospitality has focussed on relevant competencies and skill sets (e.g. Chung-Herrera, Enz & Lankau, 2003; Johanson et al., 2011; MBECS, 2011).

A group of leading academics, including Glenn Bowdin, Matthew Gonzalez, Janet Landey, Kathy Nelson, Julia Rutherford Silvers, Joe Goldblatt and William O'Toole (EMBOK, 2017), introduced a conceptual framework of creating an Event Management Body of Knowledge (EMBOK) back in 2003. This framework has created a model that hopes to *"facilitate the ability to map, define and align current event management standards consistent with the needs of a global event management environment"* (Rutherford Silvers et al., 2006, p. 185). The EMBOK model takes into account the skill set of the industry but is largely concerned with the identification of knowledge domains and the event planning process.

We are now, arguably, in a very different world to the one in which the EMBOK was originally developed. Despite this, and despite its conceptual nature, this piece of work is seen as an important tool by many leading authors – it is quoted by Bowdin, Allen, O'Toole, Harris and McDonnell (2011) and Bladen, Kennell, Abson and Wilde (2018) in their key textbooks, for example. And it was produced by a group of the most established events academics, so it certainly has credence from an academic perspective. It provides an incredibly detailed conceptual framework of the knowledge needed in event management and event studies and it avoids the trap of reducing the role of event manager to a list of skills that the other standards fall into.

Specific event competencies

There is one document which attempts to set out all of the competencies required to be an event manager – the Meetings and Business Event Competency Standards (or the MBECS). They were originally developed by the Canadian Tourism Human Resource Council and EMBOK partners in 2009, and adapted by the Meetings Professional International (MPI) and industry representatives in 2011, who turned them into a set of standard competencies specifically for meeting and business event professionals. The MBECS are intended to give the industry a benchmark to measure excellence in event management. They provide a comprehensive summary of the range of knowledge, skills and abilities required of those who work in careers planning and producing meetings and events (Cecil et al., 2013).

The standards were written in collaboration with an international stakeholder group and key phases included research and analysis of documentation relating to event management, benchmarking of a variety of foreign and national qualifications and occupational standards and the creation and validation of the competency framework (EMICS, 2009). This framework was validated through consultations and quantitative research to determine relevance, frequency and criticality ratings. The standards can be used to benefit a number of groups or individuals. For example, it is suggested that the standards are for:

♦ Event managers to plan their professional development and recognise the range of skills they need;

♦ Employers who need to define job requirements and recruit and manage an events workforce;

♦ Education providers to benchmark their curriculum and explore areas of research.

The size and scope of the standards is both impressive and intimidating – in total, the standards run to 67 pages, and list 12 domains, 33 tasks, almost 100 subtasks and 985 skill statements / abilities (Cecil et al., 2013; Rutherford-Silvers, 2010). This represents an overwhelming number of competencies, many of which are fairly generic and whilst the standards are interesting in scope, scale and detail, they are heavily reliant on technical and administrative elements and the tangible skills needed to do the job.

There are many that therefore say that documents like these produce a reductive view of a complex job role, that is built around a task-orientated job analysis (Chen et al., 2007; Wheelahan, 2007) rather than the perhaps more rounded approach of a person-orientated job analysis that results in competencies expressed as personal skills, characteristics and behaviours (Sandwith, 1993)

This reduction of a job role to a list of skills may reflect the demand from industry for a list of competencies that define and drive performance (Wheelahan, 2007; Wilson, Lenssen & Hind, 2006) but it fails to take into account the debates around the effectiveness of competency studies that have ensued since McClelland (1973) first suggested that competency could support the assessment of personnel (Grezda, 2005). These debates centre the issues posed by reducing a body of knowledge to a list of skills that don't change with context or with the future of the organisation (Turnbull, 2011; Wheelahan, 2007; Zaccaro & Horn, 2003) and that competency models are often either overwhelming in number or incredibly generic, looking very similar, even across different organisations and sectors (Turnbull, 2011).

Using competencies as a lens through which to understand how event managers lead is one of the only leadership areas that have received attention from event scholars. Indeed, I have conducted some research into this area myself (Abson, 2017) – for my research, I used Dulewicz and Higgs (2005) LDQ model in order to identify the key leadership practices for event managers working within the business events industry. The LDQ model is based on the competency school proposition that leadership requires emotional intelligence, managerial competence and intellectual competencies – it consists of 15 leadership dimensions that can be used to explain the performance of managers in an organisational context. The findings from this study established that there are six key leadership practices that are essential for the development of successful event managers. These are presented in Table 6.1 – note the mixture of technical, intelligent and emotional competencies.

As is often the case, it is useful to look at tourism and hospitality studies in order to highlight the similarities in the research approaches found in the three inter-related fields. In the same way as we have seen in events, but in far greater volumes, much of the research into leadership within tourism and hospitality falls within the managerial competence framework – they evaluate skills and competencies based on perspectives of key stakeholders, such as industry, guests, educators and students (Johanson et al., 2011). There have been numerous studies that attempt to explore competencies and leadership in hospitality – most of these focus on hotels, and at hospitality management in a particular cultural context (Bharwani & Jauhari, 2013; Harper, Brown & Wilson, 2005; Hsu & Gregory, 1995; Jeou-Shyan et al., 2011; Koenigsfeld et al., 2011; e.g. Li, Tse & Xie, 2007; Nelson & Dobson, 2001). These studies have resulted in a considerable body of knowledge on the competencies required by managers in order to lead in the context of hospitality. Their findings suggest that the need for operational and technical skills has decreased at the same time that strategic and corporate skills have increased, and that management style needs to incorporate leadership rather than just supervision (Johanson et al., 2011).

Managerial competencies

Engaging communication
Engages others and wins their support through communication tailored for each audience. Is approachable and accessible.

Resource management
Organizes resources and coordinates them efficiently and effectively. Establishes clear objectives. Converts long-term goals into action plans.

Intellectual competencies

Strategic perspectives
Sees the wider issues and broader implications. Balances short- and long-term considerations and identifies opportunities and threats.

Critical analysis and judgement
Gathering relevant information from a wide range of sources, probing the facts, and identifying advantages and disadvantages. Sound judgements and decisions making, awareness of the impact of any assumptions made.

Emotional intelligence competencies

Emotional resilience
Capability for consistent performance in a range of situations. Retain focus on a course of action or need for results in the face of personal challenge or criticism.

Interpersonal sensitivity
Be aware of, and take account of, the needs and perceptions of others in arriving at decisions and proposing solutions to problems and challenges.

Table 6.1: Six key leadership practices for event managers (Abson, 2017) with descriptions from Dulewicz and Higg's LDQ (2005)

Summary

The bewildering number of competencies required or lists of skills and personal qualities expected in order to be a leader in one particular job role makes the practical use of these lists almost impossible. In addition, they fail to take into account the way that people use these competencies or apply these skills, or the context within which they use them. As Petrie (2014, p. 10) summarised, *"For a long time we thought leadership development was working out what competencies a leader should possess and then helping individual managers to develop them – much as a bodybuilder tries to develop different muscle groups"*. But the competency model began to seem out-dated when understanding of the variety of ways people can develop grew and as scholars began to move away from the notion that leadership is all about what one person does, knows or behaves. What this body of work does tell us, however, is that we have a pretty good understanding of what people need to do in order to be a 'good' event manager.

Leadership in action: Industry insight from David Strafford, Director, Hopper Events

David is a director of Hopper Events Ltd, (www.hopper.uk) a Sheffield-based events management agency, whose previous and current projects include events with the BBC, C-Beebies, Disney on Ice, Nivea, Campo Viejo and Hull UK City of Culture 2017. He is an experienced event professional, with over 20 years in the events industry and has managed events all over the UK, in town and city centre locations, as well as greenfield sites, parks and festivals. He is a Technical Member of IOSH, a Senior Lecturer in Events Management at Sheffield Hallam University, with a Masters in International Events & Conference Management, and is a fellow of the Higher Education Academy. David has published two book chapters, a journal article and won two university Inspirational Teaching Awards for his teaching quality.

Although I am an academic, I have always worked in industry and I am still a director of an events agency. It was always my philosophy when I had a team of assistant event managers working for me, to try as best as I could to inspire my team to become genuine leaders themselves. And of course each of my team were different people, with different demands and different needs and wants in the workplace. My approach was to get to know them, understand what motivated them and work alongside them, discovering the best ways to inspire them. Reflecting on my time in industry, what makes me most proud is to see my old assistants now in positions of leadership themselves. Good event leaders should aim to create and inspire other good event leaders, rather than simply managing staff and generating followers.

The Health and Safety Executive has a definition of competence, which I rather like. They say to be a truly competent professional in your field of work then you need to have, in equal measure, skills, knowledge, experience and training.

But does that apply to event leadership? Can you become a competent leader in the world of events leadership without all four of skill, knowledge, experience and training? You can learn knowledge – and subsequently gain qualifications – in the classroom of course, and it is critical that as event managers, we understand theoretical business models, know what the legislation says, or how to write proper SMART objectives for example.

But can we be become great event leaders through studying alone? Surely to lead others we need to influence and persuade people, bring them on side and take them with us on a journey? The skills we develop over time when we are actually running events, help us learn these essential skills – we have to learn through experience.

I also like Malcom Gladwell's 10,000 hour rule from his book *Outliers*, which suggests you do not have world-class expertise of any skill until you have 10,000 hours of experience of actually doing it. This applies whether you want to become a dentist or a sushi chef, you must put the hours in and gain the experience. We event leaders need to be able to present and pitch ideas, or report feedback, at senior management or client level. But we also need to be able to influence event contractors, persuade event workers and inspire volunteers. Event leadership involves having the ability to persuade the CEO to invest in your project, whilst also liaising with clients and dealing with local authorities. And it also means knowing how to convince the security staff to work an extra hour on a cold night, or persuade the fencing delivery driver to drop the fence exactly where you want it, not just where is easiest for them. So yes, you can have management training in the classroom, but knowing how to communicate – and to persuade – at all levels in order to lead complex real world projects, is a skill best learned through experience.

It's this combination of knowledge, skills and experience which create great event leaders. It cannot be underestimated how critical interpersonal skills are in the world of event leadership; indeed bringing all of your stakeholders on board, from the boardroom to the event site, is critical to success.

Study questions

1 Explain why a list of competencies for event managers might be useful for each of the following groups:

 ◊ Event professionals

 ◊ Students

 ◊ Event academics

 ◊ Human resource directors

 ◊ Training managers.

2 Many argue that a list of competencies for event managers is reductive and therefore problematic. Why do you think this is?

3 Find a copy of the MBECS – do you think there is anything missing from the list?

4 What is the difference between a managerial, intellectual and emotional competency?

5 Looking at the list of leadership competencies identified as important by Abson (2017), identify which ones you think you already have and which ones you need to develop. How will you go about developing these competencies?

Further reading

Abson, E. (2017). How event managers lead: applying competency school theory to event management. *Event Management,* **21**(4), 403-419.

Cecil, A., Fenich, G.G., Krugman, C. & Hashimoto (2013) Review and analysis of the new international meeting and business events competency standards. *Journal of Convention & Event Tourism,* **14**(1), 65-74

Koenigsfeld, J. P., Perdue, J., Youn, H. & Woods, R., H. (2011). The changing face of competencies for club managers. *International Journal of Contemporary Hospitality Management,* **23**(7), 902-922. doi:10.1108/09596111111167524

References

Abson, E. (2017). How event managers lead: applying competency school theory to event management. *Event Management,* **21**(4), 403-419.

Athey, T. & Orth, M. (1999). Emerging competency methods for the future. *Human Resource Management* **38**(3), 215-226.

Bharwani, S. & Jauhari, V. (2013). An exploratory study of competencies required to co-create memorable customer experiences in the hospitality industry. *International Journal of Contemporary Hospitality Management,* **25**(6), 823-843.

Bladen, C., Kennell, J., Abson, E. & Wilde, N. (2018). *Events Management: An introduction* (2nd ed.). Oxon: Routledge.

Bowdin, G. A. J., Allen, J., O'Toole, W., J, Harris, R. & McDonnell, I. (2011). *Events Management* (3rd ed.). London: Butterworth-Heinemann.

Boyatzis, R. E. (1982). *The Competent Manager: A model for effective performance.* New York: John Wiley & Sons.

Boyatzis, R. E. (2009). Competencies as a behavioral approach to emotional intelligence. *Journal of Management Development,* **28**(9), 749-770.

Cecil, A., Fenich, G.G., Krugman, C. & Hashimoto (2013) Review and analysis of the new international meeting and business events competency standards. *Journal of Convention & Event Tourism,* **14**(1), 65-74

Chen, G., Kirkman, B. L., Kanfer, R., Allen, D. & Rosen, B. (2007). A multilevel study of leadership, empowerment, and performance in teams. *Journal of Applied Psychology,* **92**(2), 331-346. doi:10.1037/0021-9010.92.2.331.

Chung-Herrera, B. G., Enz, C. A. & Lankau, M. J. (2003). Grooming future hospitality leaders: A competencies model. *Cornell Hotel and Restaurant Administration Quarterly,* **44**(3), 17-25. doi:10.1016/S0010-8804(03)90266-7.

Clarke, N. (2012). Leadership in projects: what we know from the literature and new insights. *Team Performance Management,* **18**(3-4), 128-148.

Dulewicz, V. & Higgs, M. (2005). Assessing leadership styles and organisational context. *Journal of Managerial Psychology,* **20**(2), 105-123.

EMBOK. (2017). History of EMBOK. Retrieved from www.embok.org.

EMICS. (2009). Events Management International Comptency Standards. Retrieved from http://emerit.ca/product/EMIO1-OL-E/en.

Grezda, M. M. (2005). In competence we trust? Addressing conceptual ambiguity. *Journal of Management Development,* **24**(6), 530-545.

Harper, S., Brown, C. & Wilson, I. (2005). Qualifications: a fast-track to hotel general manager? *International Journal of Contemporary Hospitality Management, 17*(1), 51-64. doi:10.1108/09596110510577671.

Hsu, J.-F. & Gregory, S. R. (1995). Developing future hotel managers in Taiwan: from an industry viewpoint. *International Journal of Hospitality Management, 14*(3), 261-269. doi:10.1016/0278-4319(95)00029-1.

Jeou-Shyan, H., Hsuan, H., Chih-Hsing, L., Lin, L. & Chang-Yen, T. (2011). Competency analysis of top managers in the Taiwanese hotel industry. *International Journal of Hospitality Management, 30*(4), 1044-1054. doi:10.1016/j.ijhm.2011.03.012.

Johanson, M., Ghiselli, R., Shea, L. & Roberts, C. (2011). Changing competencies of hospitality leaders: A 25-Year review. *Journal of Hospitality & Tourism Education, 23*(3), 43-47. doi:10.1080/10963758.2011.10697012.

Koenigsfeld, J. P., Perdue, J., Youn, H. & Woods, R., H. (2011). The changing face of competencies for club managers. *International Journal of Contemporary Hospitality Management, 23*(7), 902-922. doi:10.1108/09596111111167524.

Li, L., Tse, E. C.-Y. & Xie, L. (2007). Hotel general manager profile in China: a case of Guangdong Province. *International Journal of Contemporary Hospitality Management, 19*(4), 263-274. doi:10.1108/09596110710747607.

MBECS. (2011). *The Meetings and Business Event Competency Standards* Ontario.

McClelland, D. (1973). Testing for comptence rather than intelligence. *American Psychologist, 28*, 1-14.

Müller, R. & Turner, R. (2010). Attitudes and leadership competences for project success. *Baltic Journal of Management, 5*(3), 307-329.

Mumford, M., Zaccaro, S. J., Connelly, M. S. & Marks, M. A. (2000b). Leadership skills: conclusions and future directions. *Leadership Quarterly, 11*(1), 155-170.

Mumford, M., Zaccaro, S. J., Harding, F. D., Jacobs, T. O. & Fleishman, E. A. (2000). Leadership skills for a changing world: solving complex social problems. *Leadership Quarterly, 11*(1), 11-35.

Nelson, A. & Dobson, L. (2001). Future of Hotel Education: required skills and knowledge for graduates of U.S. hospitality programs beyond the year 2000. *Journal of Hospitality & Tourism Education, 13*(5), 58-64.

Petrie, N. (2014). Future trends in leadership development: White paper. *Centre for Creative Leadership (CCL).*

Rutherford Silvers, J., Bowdin, G. A. J., O'Toole, W., J. & Beard Nelson, K. (2006) Towards an International Event Management Body of Knowledge (EMBOK). *Event Management,* **9**(4), 185-198.

Sandwith, P. (1993). A hierarchy of management training requirements: The competency domain model. *Public Personnel Management,* **22**(1), 43-62.

Schedlitzki, D. & Edwards, G. (2018). *Studying Leadership: Traditonal and critical approaches* (2nd ed.). London: Sage.

Turnbull, J. (2011). *Leadership in Context: Lessons from new leadership theory and current leadership development practice.* London: Kings Fund.

Wheelahan. (2007). How competency-based training locks the working class out of powerful knowledge: a modified Bernsteinian analysis. *British Journal of Sociological Education,* **28**(5), 627-651. doi:10.1080/01425690701505540.

Wilson, A., Lenssen, G. & Hind, P. (2006). *Leadership Qualities and Management Comptencies for Corporate Responsibility.* Berkhamsted: Ashridge / EABIS.

Zaccaro, S. J. & Horn, Z. N. (2003). Leadership theory and practice: fostering effective symbiosis. *Leadership Quarterly,* **14**(6), 769-806.

7 Knowledge and event leadership

Jane Tattersall

Chapter aims

- ☐ Introduce and critically discuss aspects of knowledge and their value
- ☐ Explore the nature and role of knowledge in events and festivals leadership
- ☐ Understand processes and challenges for tacit knowledge management
- ☐ Consider methods of tacit knowledge transfer in small and medium sized event and festival organisations
- ☐ Focus on leadership in action – knowledge management in small to medium sized enterprises.

Introduction

The aim of this chapter is to explain the value and management of different types of knowledge in an events or music festival business setting, where its potential to maximise profit and help an organisation to outperform its rivals has received less attention in academic literature than other sectors such as manufacturing or information technology. Competition in the events and festivals sectors has increased considerably as more companies join the market, and the nature and scope of events has widened to satisfy consumer appetites for more diverse and engaging experiences. Leaders that nurture, recognise, manage and employ knowledge effectively are more likely to be innovative and successful in their sector. Throughout the chapter, knowledge is explored mostly through the lens of music festivals, although the points made are easily applicable to the wider events, tourism and leisure sectors.

"Merely mentioning 'knowledge' raises problems, for anyone with the temerity to write about knowledge has to confront the pervasive disagreement about what constitutes knowledge." (Starbuck, 2006: 74)

Knowledge can be considered in many ways; what we know, how we know it, our beliefs about what is true, how our actions are led by our knowledge, and how what we do creates new knowledge. Philosophers have argued for centuries about whether we can truly 'know' anything, and the debate will continue because knowledge, understanding, truth and belief are interrelated concepts that are open to interpretation depending on a person's perspectives, experiences and environment.

Consider the following questions:

- If you believe something to be true, is it true for everyone?
- Does knowing something mean you understand it?
- Does knowing how a bicycle works make you a competent cyclist?

You may be relieved that this chapter does not debate the different philosophical stances on what knowledge is but does explore aspects of knowledge that can contribute to personal and organisational success.

The value of knowledge

Fierce rivalry is one of the conditions of a highly competitive environment. Most festivals compete using a differentiation strategy (Porter, 1985) meaning organizations need to be evermore creative and innovative in managing their resources, to give attendees unique and memorable experiences to outperform their rivals or even to survive (Johnson et al., 2014).

As a resource, knowledge is said to be more valuable than other tangible resources (such as funding, premises or stock of products) as the primary source of creating value and sustaining superior performance (Grant, 1996; Wang, Wang & Liang, 2014). Through the lens of the knowledge economy *"a firm's intellectual capital represents the only sustainable source of competitive advantage"* (Grace & Butler, 2005: 56). Providing it remains within the organization, knowledge can be a distinctive resource that is valuable, rare, non-substitutable and inimitable, creating opportunities for competitive advantage (Barney & Clark, 2007;

Johnson et al., 2014). Furthermore, it is tacit knowledge, rather than the manipulation of other available tangible resources, that is said to be the primary basis of core competencies and the key to superior performance (Lubit, 2001).

Generally, in academic literature tacit knowledge is referred to as that which cannot easily be explained or communicated in written format and comes from experience, personal perceptions and values (Werner, Dickson & Hyde, 2015). It is related to intuition and the development of skills (Ambrosini & Bowman, 2001; Taylor, 2007) and knowing how to do things. In 1955, referring to executives, Katz first suggested that what someone can accomplish in an organization is a more important consideration than the traits or personality characteristics they possess (Katz, 1974).

More specifically, it is the set of core skills employed by leaders and managers in pursuit of organizational objectives that is significant, and the combination of skills and knowledge determine what can be accomplished (Peterson & van Fleet, 2004). Furthermore, organizational learning does not occur as new insights are gained about an issue or problem but for learning to take place, action must occur (Moingeon & Edmondson, 1996). This suggests that only when insights gained from 'knowing that' are interpreted and turned into 'know how' is new knowledge created.

This aspect of workplace competence is prevalent in literature in the context of leadership and management (Kotter, 1999; Mintzberg, 2004; Northouse, 2015) but specifically addressed in relation to the skills of event managers by Bladen, Kennell, Abson, and Wilde (2012). They categorize event managers' personal & professional effectiveness as intellectual, emotional and managerial skills. Included within the intellectual category are critical analysis and judgement, vision and imagination, and strategic perspective, and each of these includes aspects of explicit and tacit knowledge.

As you will have understood from the previous chapters and the definition of Yukl (2010: 8) presented in Chapter 1, *"Leadership is the process of influencing others to understand and agree about what needs to be done and how to do it, and the process of facilitating individual and collective efforts to accomplish shared objectives."* You will also have understood that leadership is viewed through the lenses of actions, behaviours and traits. To efficiently lead, it is essential to understand where expertise, knowledge and skills are held in organisations, teams and individuals, and to create opportunities for these to be employed with maximum effectiveness to achieve the organisation's objectives. The term *knowledge management* is given to these processes and is explored further in the chapter.

Aspects of knowledge

Creating new knowledge is vital to new innovation and product development (Shankar et al., 2013) and success is far more likely to be achieved by pursuing continuous knowledge creation, diffused throughout the organization and adopted rapidly into new products and technologies (Corner & Pavlovich, 2016; Lyles, 2014; Nonaka & Takeuchi, 1995; Von Krogh, Nonaka & Ichijo, 1997). Therefore, knowledge is one of the most significant resources an organisation can utilise in remaining competitive or gaining an advantage over rivals. Lindner and Wald (2011) suggest that:

- ◆ Knowledge exists in people's heads.

- ◆ It includes skills and experience as well as facts retained.

- ◆ Some knowledge can be shared with others.

- ◆ It depends on people's views and perspectives of the world.

Much that has been written about knowledge in the context of individual and organisation performance, does not differentiate between information and experience, facts and skills, but addresses the resource 'knowledge' as one concept. This holistic view of knowledge, whilst not incorrect, does not take into account the issues associated with sharing and understanding different types of knowledge. For example, it is easy to email ticket sales data to a colleague but interpreting the data and understanding its implications for the delivery of an event requires analytical skills and experience that are less easy to acquire and execute. In the following sections, knowledge is disseminated so readers can appreciate the value of, and challenges associated with its different aspects.

Perspectives of knowledge that seek to explain its different types and aspects are often expressed as dichotomies.

The explicit – tacit knowledge continuum

"We know more than we can tell" Michael Polanyi (1967).

The most common distinction made in literature is that between explicit and tacit knowledge. In plain terms, explicit knowledge is that which can be expressed in formal language, presented numerically, explained, classified, written down and stored in a database by individuals to share with other individuals or teams. Explicit knowledge is linked with information and in events and festival organisations, this can include business plans, event plans, operational documents, site plans, project management documents, operating systems, client and attendee details, entertainer information and riders, financial information and anything else which can be expressed in words and numbers and is able to be communicated though documents and conversations.

Tacit knowledge is generalised to be that which cannot easily be explained or communicated in written format and comes from experience, personal perceptions and values and is context dependent (Werner, Dickson & Hyde, 2015). It is related to intuition and the development of skills (Ambrosini & Bowman, 2001; Taylor, 2007) and knowing how to do things. In events and festival organisations this can include 'knowing' what will work on a proposed event site, 'knowing' how to respond to an unforeseen problem or situation or producing creative ideas for installations.

Michael Polanyi is widely recognised as introducing the concept of tacit knowledge, and the explicit–tacit continuum in 1966 (Zander & Kogut, 1995; Leonard & Sensiper, 1998; Ambrosini & Bowman, 1991; Bhardwaj & Monin, 2006; Gascoigne & Thornton, 2013; Muskat & Deery, 2017), following his earlier work on personal knowledge in 1958. He identified the difference between explicit 'knowing what' at one end of the continuum and tacit 'knowing how' knowledge at the opposite end. Polanyi's fundamental argument is that it may not be possible to objectively or explicitly formalise all knowledge, due to the inability of people to put into words some of the knowledge they hold in their heads. It is not a straightforward case of either/or.

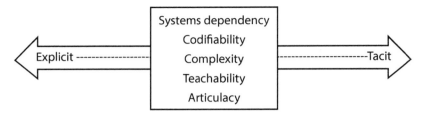

Figure 7.1: The Explicit – Tacit continuum

Zander and Kogut (1995) further explored the dimensions of explicit – tacit knowledge and proposed four characteristics of knowledge to consider in understanding how to manage different types of knowledge:

- **Codifiability** – the degree to which knowledge can be represented by symbols;
- **Teachability** – the degree to which knowledge can be taught;
- **Complexity** – the degree to which knowledge embodies multiple kinds of competencies;
- **Systems dependence** – the degree to which knowledge requires many different experienced people for its application.

Tacit and explicit knowledge interact, and knowledge creation relies on the interaction of both. Furthermore, there is always a tacit element of explicit knowledge (Leonard & Sensiper, 1998; Panahi, Watson & Partridge, 2016) insofar as the comprehension of explicit knowledge requires some implicit understanding of how to act upon it. Even after it is shared, an element of knowledge always remains tacit (Muñoz et al., 2015). Explicit knowledge is accessible and articulable to others, structured, codified, objective, rational and created in the 'there and then' whereas tacit elements are subjective, experiential, held in people's heads, semi-conscious or unconscious and created in the 'here and now' (Leonard & Sensiper, 1998).

If important knowledge remains tacit, this can result in learned lessons being lost, mistakes being made or repeated, work duplicated or wasted, ideas or solutions not shared, experience and skills not developed, all with implications for productivity, creativity and motivation. Missed opportunities for recognising, appreciating and sharing tacit knowledge are common hindrances for many individuals and organisations, as it usually involves face to face contact and potentially costly and time-consuming interventions (Puusa & Eerikainen, 2010).

Companies may also face significant losses if valuable tacit knowledge leaves with employees who retire or move on (Jennex, 2014), as is inevitable in the business cycle, and leaders and managers should consider actions to try to recognise and capture the resource before it is too late.

Private and public knowledge

Private knowledge, that which is contained or is proprietary to the organization (Chua, 2002) can be a source of competitive advantage if it is analysed and found to be valuable, rare, inimitable and non-substitutable (Barney, 1991). Public knowledge, on the other hand, such as best practice, health and safety legislation, sustainability and generic ways of organizing events (or events organizations), that were once private knowledge, are not considered sources of competitive advantage as they are not unique to the organization (Chua, 2002).

Personal and collective knowledge

Personal knowledge can be viewed from two epistemological perspectives of possession and practice (Razmerita, Kirchner & Nabeth, 2014). Where personal knowledge is possessed, it is an intangible personal asset and cognitive capacity. The practice view relates knowledge to actions, to what people do, which can also be interpreted as skill. Collective knowledge, or organizational knowledge is used to mean the total knowledge, explicit and tacit that is common to all members of a team or organization, and can relate to knowledge of mission, vision, rules, regulations, procedures (Taylor, 2007) or 'invisible structure' (Razmerita et al., 2014: 76).

Collective knowledge is prioritized by some as a strategic asset over individual knowledge as it is transformed to become organizational wisdom through shared experiences, competencies and expertise (Bollinger and Smith, 2001; Chua, 2002).

Sharing and retention of tacit knowledge are discussed further in the chapter, but as with the broader concept of knowledge, tacit knowledge itself has more than one dimension.

Aspects of tacit knowledge

Implicit and latent knowledge

Taylor (2007) observed that the term tacit knowledge is often over simplified, used to mean any knowledge which is not written down, and this leads to ambiguity or misconception about what it is and whether it can, in fact, be captured.

Misunderstandings, generalizations and ambiguity can occur when the term tacit knowledge is used interchangeably with implicit or latent knowledge, both types of knowledge that can be articulated but has not yet been (Agrawal, 2006) and often it is these types of knowledge that several articles refer to when discussing tacit knowledge in a generalised way, to mean any knowledge which is not written down, verbalised or easy to explain (Taylor, 2007).

These distinctions may appear pedantic, but the implications for accessing and sharing this knowledge are significant, if leaders can find ways to gain insights into where previously uncommunicated knowledge, skill or know-how experience resides and devise ways to address the issue.

Implicit knowledge

Muñoz et al. (2015) consider a typical company boardroom meeting, which could be a scenario in any events or festival organization. Here, some knowledge is available explicitly as financial reports, market research or other types of information. Some knowledge is not explicit at the time of the meeting but can be made explicit by executives participating in the meeting verbally sharing informal data that is not written or recorded in formal reports. This knowledge, that was not formerly explicit but is subsequently shared, is interpreted by Frappaolo (2008) as implicit knowledge. Authors frequently generalise this type of knowledge as tacit in academic literature.

Latent knowledge

This term was proposed by Agrawal (2006:64) in his examination of the outcomes of experiments conducted by inventors at universities. He found that potentially valuable knowledge, resulting from failed experiments, was being lost. According to his respondents, most of their experiments failed or partially failed, but due to the constrains of time and funding, the results were not codified. This knowledge, he claims, is not tacit knowledge as it could have be codified but at the time was not. Agrawal states that this latent knowledge *"is valuable for climbing atop the shoulders of giants, advancing research, and, in the case of commercialization, developing the early-stage inventions into saleable products or processes"*. Making efforts to uncover latent knowledge in event organizations could have significant implications for the health, safety and enjoyment of attendees, where on-site changes have been made in real time but not recorded.

Supporting this point, Muskat and Deery (2017: 438) conducted qualitative research with event organisers or managers to ascertain the level and processes used to transfer knowledge during the pre-event, event and post-event stages events and identified that in the pre-event phase, there is great reliance on written, explicit knowledge pertaining to manuals and checklists and that event staff *"seek tacit knowledge via face-to-face delivery"*. They further conclude that *"tacit knowledge evolves during the event, but often remains hidden and stuck with the knowledge holder"* (Muskat & Deery, 2017:445). Discerning between the dimensions of tacit knowledge can inform strategies for its management and designing activities to maximise its value in the context in which it arises.

Generalisations or ambiguous use of the term 'tacit knowledge' are unhelpful in planning knowledge sharing activities, because as we have seen, latent or implicit knowledge is easier to voice than knowledge that sits at the most tacit end of the continuum. Depending on organisational or project needs, knowledge management activities should be tailored and designed to consider the type of knowledge required to be shared.

Knowledge management

Having gained an understanding of the different types and aspects of knowledge, readers may ask themselves "what should event leaders do to make the most of it?" Academics and industry professionals continue to debate this and as with aspects of leadership, perspectives vary and are context and resource dependent. Therefore, understanding who possesses what knowledge, and the distribution, use and adoption processes that exist or not in the company is critical in developing knowledge management strategies. Paradoxically, knowledge of knowledge management will determine how successfully an organisation is able to utilise all the knowledge held within the heads of its people.

As a concept, knowledge management has been extensively researched and published since the early 1990s, not only in dedicated knowledge or management text books and journals but also in other fields of research such as information technology and economics (Arisha, 2013) and more recently in hospitality, tourism and events journals (see Singh, Racherla & Hu, 2007; Hallin & Marnburg, 2008; Morgan, 2008; Shaw & Williams, 2009; Ragsdell & Jepson, 2014; Stadler, Fullagar & Reid, 2014; Stadler & Fullagar, 2016). A large volume of work appeared to emerge as a ready-made concept, adopted initially by the manufacturing industries during the 1990s (Lambe, 2011), and despite some warnings that knowledge management was simply a fad in the field of information systems the concept has clearly endured and remains a much debated topic of contemporary literature with new methods and practices still put forward (Grant, 2016).

Definitions of knowledge management are numerous, but generally it is acknowledged that to be successful, the process should be conducted at all levels of an organisation and involve four main stages, mainly referred to as:

♦ Knowledge creation, capture or acquisition;

♦ Knowledge sharing, distribution or coordination;

♦ Knowledge use, adoption or implementation;

♦ Knowledge storage or organisational memory.

Jimenez-Jimenez & Sanz Valle (2011) emphasise the importance of managing and leveraging knowledge assets for organizational success:

♦ Knowledge acquisition is the process used by an organisation to obtain new information and knowledge.

♦ Knowledge distribution is the process by which information is shared by employees.

♦ Knowledge interpretation occurs when information in given meaning and is transformed into new common knowledge

♦ Organisational memory is the method by which the information and knowledge are stored for use in the future.

Each of these stages present their own challenges and are explored later in the chapter.

Hallin and Marnbarg (2008) address the importance of individual and group knowledge and their role in innovation, one of the building blocks of competitive advantage and organisation success (Hill, Jones & Schilling, 2015):

> *"Knowledge Management may be understood as the practice of capturing and developing individual and collective knowledge within an organization for the purpose of using it to promote innovation through the transfer of knowledge and continuous learning"*
> (Hallin and Marnbarg, 2008: 367).

The process clearly requires management and if we follow Kotterman (2006), it is a leader who recognises the importance of knowledge management and motivates others to engage with it and empowers them to recognise, value and make use of their own and others' knowledge. In practice, however, knowledge management initiatives are not so straightforward and the failure rate is high. Governance and leadership, culture, strategy, lack of knowledge management understanding, IT and measurement issues are common reasons for poor results (Ribiere & Calabrese, 2017).

Responsibility for getting these aspects right lies with leaders and managers, but it is not simply a question of having access to the right plan and implementing it:

> *'"Knowledge, by itself, is worthless. It is the strategic use of this knowledge, coupled with a sense of entrepreneurs hip that enables individuals, teams, and organizations to hone their creativity, so that they can meet and even surpass their goals."*
> (Phipps & Prieto, 2012)

If success in business (think also love and life) was achievable by simply 'knowing' what to do to achieve it, there would be many more (blissfully happy) billionaires in the world. A search for 'How to be successful at…' on Amazon UK returned 6000 over titles (August, 2020), each claiming to share with the reader the secret to success in any number of areas including careers, social skills, making big money, leading organisations, being a youtuber, selling cars, winning interviews or finding the love of their life. Clearly, there is more to it than having information on what to do to be successful. There is always a personal interpretation of the information, based on experience, understanding and resource.

Leaders should know where knowledge sits in their organisation, and if they do not, they will be less able to motivate and steer the people they lead to achieve their objectives. Every function of an organisation requires knowledge (explicit and tacit) to flow efficiently and effectively, and the processes of knowledge sharing and knowledge transfer have been widely commented upon in academic and industry literature.

Barriers and challenges

The difficulties experienced by organizations in managing and exploiting knowledge can be viewed from the perspective of a theoretical understanding of the processes required or a practice-based view of the mechanics, but human nature and organisation culture also play a role.

Knowledge hiding, withholding or concealing task information, ideas or know-how knowledge are not unusual in organizations and can inhibit individual or organizational performance (Huo et al., 2016). This phenomenon is linked to employees feeling a strong ownership of their knowledge and resisting sharing it, to obtain or maintain status or power (Peng, 2013). An interesting contrast is put forward by Huo et al. (2016: 892) between 'knowledge hiding', which is intentional and 'knowledge hoarding' which may result from a lack of time, poor procedures or other unforeseen conditions. They found that when the perceived value of the knowledge and the level of cooperation needed is high, knowledge hiding was less prevalent and that perceptions of 'organizational justice' were also influential. From a slightly different perspective Vitari, Moro, Ravarini and Bourdon (2007) found that appropriate rewards systems and the definition of the organizational structure have the potential to significantly increase acceptance of knowledge management systems.

Barriers to implementing knowledge management activities may include the following, summarised in Table 7.1.

There are clearly significant challenges to overcome from an organisation and individual perspective, to create an environment where people feel confident and willing to engage in knowledge management activities. A good place to start is with commitment from leaders to generate knowledge strategies and create opportunities to implement them.

7: Knowledge and event leadership

Some studies have focused on methods used for tacit knowledge transfer, but the distinction between implicit, latent or tacit knowledge is not always apparent.

Table 7.1: Barriers to implementing knowledge management activities (From Bollinger and Smith, 2001)

Organizational perspective
- Time consuming
- Labour intensive
- People are busy
- Temporary project teams
- Workers see no benefit
- Difficult to codify tacit knowledge
- Strong positive culture is needed for people to care enough
- May involve additional work

Team/group perspective
- Reward for individual effort will encourage hoarding of knowledge
- Fear of recrimination and criticism from peers and management
- Lack of respect for other disciplines
- Lack of respect, trust and common goal

Individual perspective
- Reluctance to share information
- Knowledge is source of power, advancement, or reward/punishment
- Sense of worth and status because of expertise
- Fear of diminished personal value if give up know-how
- Competition among professionals

Summary

This chapter has presented an argument for recognising knowledge, and in particular dimensions of tacit knowledge, as a valuable and often underappreciated resource of event and festival organisations. Tacit knowledge has been subdivided into implicit (unshared), latent (dormant) and tacit (inarticulable) knowledge, with implications where leaders take the time to recognise it and create opportunities for sharing and developing it successfully within organisations. Uncovering implicit and latent knowledge is more easily achieved through improved, focused interaction between people to improve innovation and efficiency and reduce mistakes. Tacit knowledge is the most elusive type, is learned through experience and cannot easily be transferred from one person to another. The instinctive and personal nature of tacit knowledge means that its holder may have advantages of power, expertise and value over others. As leadership is about maximising organisational performance, understanding tacit knowledge and its value to individuals and leaders, can enhance our personal and career development, whilst helping to future proof events and festival organisations.

Leadership in action: Knowledge management in small and medium sized enterprises

This industry insight is based on research by Jane Tattersall

The size of an organisation can impact on the successful management of knowledge. Larger corporate event organizations such as Live Nation (Music) UK Ltd deliver festivals and other music events in the UK. In 2019, they employed 287 employees and posted an annual turnover in of over £276m (FAME, 2021) and as such, perform many organisational functions using in-house teams, providing a relatively stable opportunity for knowledge management projects to take place.

Business models in smaller organisations that rely on freelancers and other processes such as co-creation and crowdsourcing, result in multiple, often temporary stakeholders. In contrast to Live Nation, many independent music festivals employ a small team of people and are examples of temporary organizations. Directors and other key contributors may have other careers that they perform outside or around the festival season. Temporary organizations are faced with one-off or annual projects, fragmentation of people and their knowledge spread between other projects (Lindner & Wald, 2011) and are therefore faced with particular challenges compared to permanent organizations such as Live Nation. Lindner and Wald (2011) consider these to be:

- ☐ Less opportunity for organizational learning or developing shared routines;
- ☐ Irregular or shifting work groups can diffuse individual or organizational knowledge;
- ☐ Difficulty in knowledge sharing opportunities due to lack of established learning processes;
- ☐ Immediacy and short-term focus can lead to insufficient time for knowledge management systems to have impact and cause insufficient knowledge transfer between projects.

The entrepreneurial nature of small and medium sized enterprises (SME) (Pérez-Luño, Saparito & Gopalakrishnan, 2016) suggests that there is a common interest in building collective tacit knowledge, achieved through the sharing of specialized, accumulated private knowledge so that it is *"refined, transformed, extended, and updated so that innovations can be achieved"* (Yuqin et al., 2012: 296). Despite this positive relationship between an SME's entrepreneurial orientation and tacit knowledge, there is a risk of losing creative vision due to the need to respond to immediate customer demands, or in other words, having to adapt current innovations in place of developing new products or services. The size and absorptive capacity of a smaller organization can have a positive influence on tacit knowledge transfer, depending on how closely the knowledge between the donor and recipient is related. Within a community of practice, people are said to share a sense of identity, have common values and share some knowledge or practice, whereas a cross-community group differs as the people or groups may have diverse identities, contexts, organizational or project boundaries. In other words, it does not necessarily follow that smaller organisations have less opportunities to share knowledge, as the closeness of working relationships may foster personal and collective knowledge but there may be fewer formalised processes to discuss or maximise its value. Leaders that recognise this can implement knowledge management activities according to their organisation's resources and their leadership skills.

Study questions

1 Discuss the differences between explicit, implicit, latent and tacit knowledge in the context of event management organisations and give examples of each.

2 Implicit and tacit knowledge are often discussed as tacit knowledge in the literature. Why is it important for events organisation to discern between the types and what are the implications and opportunities associated with this?

3 What are the main barriers for successful knowledge transfer and what can leaders do about them?

4 What aspects of leadership do you associate with the most tacit type of knowledge? Give two examples and outline how a leader could transfer this knowledge to someone else.

5 Do you think larger event organisations are likely to be more or less successful at knowledge management than smaller or medium sized operations and explain why.

6 What are the main benefits to individuals of exploring their tacit knowledge?

Further Reading

Gascoigne, N. & Thornton, T. (2013). *Tacit Knowledge* Acumen.

Nonaka, I., Toyama, R. & Konno, N. (2000). SECI, ba and leadership: A unified model of dynamic knowledge creation. *Long Range Planning,* **33**(1), 5-34. doi:10.1016/S0024-6301(99)00115-6

Stadler, R. & Fullagar, S. (2016). Appreciating formal and informal knowledge transfer practices within creative festival organizations. *Journal of Knowledge Management, 20*(1), 146-161.

References

Agrawal, A. (2006). Engaging the inventor: Exploring licensing strategies for university inventions and the role of latent knowledge. *Strategic Management Journal,* **27**(1), 63-79. doi:10.1002/smj.508.

Ambrosini, V. & Bowman, C. (2001). Tacit knowledge: Some suggestions for operationalization. *Journal of Management Studies,* **38**(6), 811-829. doi:10.1111/1467-6486.00260.

Arisha, A. (2013). Knowledge management and measurement: A critical review. *Journal of Knowledge Management,* **17**(6), 873-901. doi:10.1108/JKM-12-2012-0381.

Barney, J. (1991). Firm resources and sustained competitive advantage. *Journal of Management,* **17**(1), 99-120.

Barney, J. B. & Clark, D. N. (2007). *Resource-Based Theory : Creating and sustaining competitive advantage.* Oxford: Oxford University Press.

Bhardwaj, M. & Monin, J. (2006). Tacit to explicit: An interplay shaping organization knowledge. *Journal of Knowledge Management,* **10**(3), 72-85. doi:10.1108/13673270610670867.

Bladen, C., Kennell, J., Abson, E. & Wilde, N.(2012). *Events Management : An introduction.* London: Routledge.

Bollinger, A. S. & Smith, R. D. (2001). Managing organizational knowledge as a strategic asset. *Journal of Knowledge Management,* **5**(1), 8-18. doi:10.1108/13673270110384365.

Chua, A. (2002). Taxonomy of organisational knowledge. *Singapore Management Review,* **24**(2), 69.

Corner, P. & Pavlovich, K. (2016). Shared value through inner knowledge creation. *Journal of Business Ethics,* **135**(3), 543-555. doi:10.1007/s10551-014-2488-x.

FAME, (2021) Company Report of Live Nation (Music) UK Limited. http://fame4.bvdinfo.com.

Frappaolo, C. (2008). Implicit knowledge. *Knowledge Management Research & Practice,* **6**(1), 23. doi:10.1057/palgrave.kmrp.8500168.

Gascoigne, N. & Thornton, T. (2013). *Tacit Knowledge* Acumen.

Grace, A. & Butler, T. (2005). Beyond knowledge management: Introducing learning management systems. *Journal of Cases on Information Technology (JCIT),* **7**(1), 53-70. doi:10.4018/jcit.2005010104.

Grant, R. (1996). Toward a knowledge- based theory of the firm. *Strategic Management Journal,* **17**, 109-122.

Grant, S. B. (2016). Classifying emerging knowledge sharing practices and some insights into antecedents to social networking: A case in insurance. *Journal of Knowledge Management,* **20**(5), 898-917.

Hallin, C. A. & Marnburg, E. (2008). Knowledge management in the hospitality industry: A review of empirical research. *Tourism Management,* **29**(2), 366-381. doi:10.1016/j.tourman.2007.02.019.

Hill, C. W. L., Jones, G. R. & Schilling, M. A.,. (2015). *Strategic Management: An integrated approach* (11th ed.) Cengage Learning.

Huo, W., Cai, Z., Luo, J., Men, C. & Jia, R. (2016). Antecedents and intervention mechanisms: A multi-level study of R&D team's knowledge hiding behavior. *Journal of Knowledge Management, 20*(5), 880-897.

Jennex, E. M. (2014). A proposed method for assessing knowledge loss risk with departing personnel. *Vine, 44*(2), 185-209.

Jiménez-Jiménez, D. & Sanz-Valle, R. (2011). Innovation, organizational learning, and performance. *Journal of Business Research, 64*(4), 408-417. doi:http://dx.doi.org.lcproxy.shu.ac.uk/10.1016/j.jbusres.2010.09.010.

Johnson, G., Whittington, R., Angwin, D., Regner, P. & Scholes, K. (2014). *Exploring Strategy* (10th ed.) Pearson Education.

Katz, R. L. (1974). Skills of an effective administrator. *Harvard Business Review*, Oct.

Kotter, J. P. (1999). *John P. Kotter on What Leaders Really Do*. Boston: Harvard Business School Press.

Lambe, P. (2011). The unacknowledged parentage of knowledge management. *Journal of Knowledge Management, 15*(2), 175-197. doi:10.1108/13673271111119646.

Leonard, D. & Sensiper, S. (1998). The role of tacit knowledge in group innovation. *California Management Review, 40*(3), 112-132. doi:10.2307/41165946.

Lindner, F. & Wald, A. (2011). Success factors of knowledge management in temporary organizations. *International Journal of Project Management, 29*(7), 877-888. doi:10.1016/j.ijproman.2010.09.003.

Lubit, R. (2001). The keys to sustainable competitive advantage: Tacit knowledge and knowledge management: *Organizational Dynamics, 29*(3), 164-178. doi:10.1016/S0090-2616(01)00026-2.

Lyles, M. A. (2014). Organizational learning, knowledge creation, problem formulation and innovation in messy problems. *European Management Journal, 32*(1), 132–136. doi:10.1016/j.emj.2013.05.003.

Mintzberg, H. (2004). *Managers not MBAs : A hard look at the soft practice of managing and management development*. San Francisco, CA: Berrett-Koehler.

Moingeon, B. & Edmondson, A. C. (1996). *Organizational Learning and Competitive Advantage*. London: SAGE.

Morgan, M. (2008). What makes a good festival? understanding the event experience. *Event Management,* **12**(2), 81-93. doi:10.3727/152599509787992562.

Muskat, B. & Deery, M. (2017). Knowledge transfer and organizational memory: An events perspective. *Event Management,* **21**(4), 431-447. doi:10.3727/152599517X14998876105765.

Muñoz, C., Mosey, S. & Binks, M. (2015). The tacit mystery: Reconciling different approaches to tacit knowledge. *Knowledge Management Research & Practice,* **13**(3), 289-298. doi:10.1057/kmrp.2013.50.

Nonaka, I. & Takeuchi, H. (1995). *The Knowledge-Creating Company : How Japanese companies create the dynamics of innovation.* Oxford University Press.

Northouse, P. G. (2015). *Leadership: Theory and practice* (7th ed.). London: SAGE.

Panahi, S., Watson, J. & Partridge, H. (2016). Information encountering on social media and tacit knowledge sharing. *Journal of Information Science,* **42**(4), 539-550. doi:10.1177/0165551515598883

Peng, H. (2013), Why and when do people hide knowledge?, *Journal of Knowledge Management,* **17**(3), 398-415.

Pérez-Luño, A., Saparito, P. & Gopalakrishnan, S. (2016). Small and medium-sized enterprises' entrepreneurial versus market orientation and the creation of tacit knowledge. *Journal of Small Business Management,* **54**(1), 262-278. doi:10.1111/jsbm.12144

Peterson, T. O. & Van Fleet, D.,D. (2004). The ongoing legacy of R.L. Katz. *Management Decision,* **42**(10), 1297-1308. doi:10.1108/00251740410568980

Phipps, S. & Prieto, L. (2012). Knowledge is power? an inquiry into knowledge management, its effects on individual creativity, and the moderating role of an entrepreneurial mindset. *Academy of Strategic Management Journal,* **11**(1), 43-57.

Polanyi, M. (1967). *The Tacit Knowledge Dimension.* London: Routledge & Kegan Paul.

Porter, M. E (1985). *The Competitive Advantage: Creating and Sustaining Superior Performance.* NY: Free Press.

Puusa, A. & Eerikäinen, M. (2010). Is tacit knowledge really tacit? *Electronic Journal of Knowledge Management,* **8**(3), 307-318.

Ragsdell, G. & Jepson, A. (2014). Knowledge sharing: Insights from campaign for real ale (CAMRA) festival volunteers. *International Journal of Event and Festival Management, 5*(3), 279-279.

Razmerita, L., Kirchner, K. & Nabeth, T. (2014). Social media in organizations: Leveraging personal and collective knowledge processes. *Journal of Organizational Computing and Electronic Commerce, 24*(1), 74-93. doi:10.1080/10919392.2014.866504

Ribière, V., & Calabrese, F. (2017). Why are companies still struggling to implement knowledge management? Answers from 34 experts in the field. In *Successes and Failures of Knowledge Management* (pp. 13–34). Elsevier Inc. https://doi.org/10.1016/B978-0-12-805187-0.00002-4

Shankar, R., Mittal, N., Rabinowitz, S., Baveja, A. & Acharia, S. (2013). A collaborative framework to minimise knowledge loss in new product development. *International Journal of Production Research, 51*(7), 2049-2059. doi:10.1080/00207543.2012.701779

Shaw, G. & Williams, A. (2009). Knowledge transfer and management in tourism organisations: An emerging research agenda. *Tourism Management, 30*(3), 325-335. doi:10.1016/j.tourman.2008.02.023.

Singh, N., Racherla, P. & Hu, C. (2007). Knowledge mapping for safe festivals and events: An ontological approach. *Event Management, 11*(1), 71-80. doi:10.3727/152599508783943264.

Stadler, R., Fullagar, S. & Reid, S. (2014). The professionalization of festival organizations: A relational approach to knowledge management. *Event Management, 18*(1), 39-52. doi:10.3727/152599514X13883555341841.

Stadler, R. & Fullagar, S. (2016). Appreciating formal and informal knowledge transfer practices within creative festival organizations. *Journal of Knowledge Management, 20*(1), 146-161.

Taylor, H. (2007). Tacit knowledge: Conceptualizations and operationalizations. *International Journal of Knowledge Management, 3*(3), 60-73. doi:10.4018/jkm.2007070104.

Vitari, C., Moro, J., Ravarini, A., & Bourdon, I. (2007). Improving KMS acceptance: the role of organizational and individuals' influence. *International Journal of Knowledge Management, 3*(2), 68–90. https://doi.org/10.4018/jkm.2007040104

Von Krogh, G., Ichijo, K. & Nonaka, I. (2000). *Enabling Knowledge Creation.* US: Oxford University Press.

Wang, Z., Wang, N. & Liang, H. (2014). Knowledge sharing, intellectual capital and firm performance. *Management Decision, 52*(2), 230-258. doi:10.1108/MD-02-2013-0064.

Werner, K., Dickson, G. & Hyde, K. F. (2015). Learning and knowledge transfer processes in a mega-events context: The case of the 2011 rugby world cup. *Tourism Management, 48*, 174-187. doi:http://dx.doi.org. lcproxy.shu.ac.uk/10.1016/j.tourman.2014.11.003.

William H. Starbuck. (2006). *The Production of Knowledge.* Oxford University Press.

Yukl, G. (2010). *Leadership in Organisations* (3rd ed.). New Jersey: Pearson.

Yuqin, Z., Guijun, W., Zhenqiang, B. & Quanke, P. (2012). A game between enterprise and employees about the tacit knowledge transfer and sharing. *Physics Procedia, 24*, 1789-1795. doi:10.1016/j.phpro.2012.02.263.

Zander, U. & Kogut, B. (1995). Knowledge and the speed of the transfer and imitation of organizational capabilities: An empirical test. *Organization Science, 6*(1), 76. doi:10.1287/orsc.6.1.76.

8 Events, leadership and power

Chapter aims

- ☐ Consider the question who leads and when?
- ☐ Explore the power of leaders
- ☐ Understand the different types of power
- ☐ Reflect on the power of events to lead change in society
- ☐ Reflect on the power of event communities
- ☐ Discuss the nature of power relationships with event stakeholders
- ☐ Focus on leadership in action: Industry insight from Carrie Abernathy of the Association for Women in Events.

Introduction

A criticism of many of the conceptualisations of leadership is that they tend to focus on the positive nature of leadership and ignore the issues of power, influence and domination (Bolden, 2011). This really is a key criticism, because when you think about it, how can leadership be untangled from the power dynamics that occur within and around it? Despite the rise in viewing leadership as an influence process, as charted in Chapters 3,4 and 5 of this book, leadership in events is still often attributed to those in formal positions of power – by that I mean those in managerial positions, who have the power to make decisions about their followers working lives, and even – at the extreme end – decide to terminate people's employment. Critics such as Bolden (2011), Alvesson and Spicer (2012) argue that when leadership is the preserve of those in managerial positions, then the dynamics of who holds the power in the relationships are always unequal, and it is impossible to overcome these inequalities, because one person is always in a stronger position than the other. This chapter therefore gives the reader a brief overview on the power of leaders in events, and an insight into both the benefits and issues of that power.

A second level of concern is also leadership within the events community – who is it that brings people and organisations together? What does it take to achieve effective collaboration among events and between events and other key stakeholders? This might be a matter of individual leaders taking charge, but equally it could be that leadership emerges from specific network dynamics. In viewing leadership as both a process of influence *and* a process of power, we can gain useful insights into the power relationships that may be at work.

Who leads, and when – and what does that have to do with power?

Whilst large parts of this book have been concerned with the democratisation of leadership, there is no denying the continued emphasis within the event industry of the role of the formal leader. Most event organisations are structured around a typical hierarchical structure, with organisational teams each managed by team leaders, and a chain of command that reaches up to a leadership team who make the strategic decisions on the vision and direction of the organisation. It is risky then for us to ignore the role of a formal leader when – in nearly every type of organisation – they are still an essential part of the structure. Indeed, as I suggested in Chapter 5, researchers now recognise that in order to fully understand leadership processes, both vertical (top-down leadership) and collective leadership throughout the organisation need to be considered (Day et al. 2004, Ensley et al. 2006).

Unlike other industries, such as banking or manufacturing, the output of the event community is based on the consumption of an experience (Pine & Gilmore 1999). What people pay for, or sign up to, isn't a tangible product and nothing can be taken away (Pernecky, 2015). This intangibility means that perceived consumer experiences are central to a successful event – but it also creates significant challenges in shaping experiences that create a lasting legacy, or changes to consumer thinking and behaviour – which are integral to successful outcomes. Similarly, experiences are also temporary in nature – they are planned for, staged and then they disappear – and this is true even of recurring event experiences (Bladen et al., 2018). This temporality results in inevitable and ever-growing pressure to deliver – there is only one chance to get things right, and mistakes in planning or delivery are very difficult to rectify when the experience is underway (Van der Wagen, 2006; Bowdin et al., 2011). And, because the work is often geared towards one particular point in time – that of the experience delivery – there is an associated, and increased, risk of job insecurity and poor working conditions, for example very long and unsocial hours. This then leads to the key issue of power – that ever-growing pressure, which culminates in that 'it has to be alright on the night' feeling, means that decisions need to get made quickly, and those that have the power to make the decisions are therefore looked to as leaders (whether they want to be or not). Ultimately during the live delivery of an event, there is usually one person with whom all the decisions rest and power is therefore enshrined in the role – what they decide to do is what will happen.

The power of leadership

What do we mean by power? Power is most commonly defined as the ability of an individual to exercise some sort of control over someone else. Leadership, on the other hand, should not be solely bound up with power – after all, an individual can have the ability to influence others, despite not being in a formal – powerful – leadership position. In other words, people with power have the ability to influence others *and* the ability to exert control over others. Leaders will have the ability to exert influence over others, but they do not necessarily have the power to make people do what they want.

This discussion of the intersection between power and leadership might then be better reframed as a discussion of power and influence. As we have seen throughout this book, leadership is most usefully conceptualised as a process of influence over other people. Many scholars therefore suggest that the group of followers give power to the leader (by accepting their leadership) and are also able to take power away if they become dissatisfied with the leaders. So, leaders must exercise their power carefully because power is simply the right to provide leadership. As Warren Bennis famously suggests, *"leadership is the wise use of power. Power is the capacity to translate intention into reality and sustain it."*

(Note: this citation is widely attributed to Bennis, but I can find no original source data. Be careful if you reuse this quotation in your assignments!)

Therefore, following this line of thinking, event leaders have power over a multitude of situations at work. That doesn't necessarily mean that they *should* use power over the people they lead – good leaders will not need to display their power in order to get results, instead they will empower others. But of course, bad leaders exist, and many will misuse their power.

But what do we mean by the power of leaders? In many ways, it is simple – power is the capacity or potential to influence (Northouse, 2015). Those in formal leadership positions have the power to make a range of decisions that will impact on the people who work for them. For example, event leader managers are the ones who usually decide:

♦ How much people get paid;

♦ Whether or not to reward staff with financial bonuses;

♦ What work each staff member will do;

♦ To allow holiday requests.

And event leaders decide things like:

♦ Who will feature on their event programme;

♦ Which supplier they will use;

♦ How much they will pay their suppliers;

♦ Which sponsor gets the best spot in the VIP lounge;

♦ Who sits where at the conference dinner.

All of these decisions have power attached to them – for those affected by them, the outcomes can be positive or negative. But there are many different types of power, and given the interconnectedness of power and leadership, it is important we understand what they are. Northouse (2015) describes five types of power, and they are explained in Table 8.1.

Legitimate power

Legitimate power is the same as authority.

Legitimate power comes from the power that a leader has because of their position in the organisation.

People with legitimate power will often also have reward, coercive and / or expert power – but legitimate power is a wider concept than these.

To understand legitimate power, think about how, if a policeman or the boss of your company tells you to do something, you are likely to do it.

Coercive power

Coercive power is the power leaders have to control, manipulate or punish.

Leaders in formal managerial positions have coercive power, because they can punish you for not doing as they ask.

To understand coercive power, think about how your line manager at work can decide to give you the most unpleasant jobs, or demote or sack you.

Reward power

Reward power is the power to give benefits or rewards.

Rewards can be financial, or emotional or motivational – basically anything the person values can act as a reward.

To understand reward power, think about how you feel when someone in a leadership positions praises you for doing a good job. Or consider how it feels to get a bonus because of your hard work!

Expert power

Expert power is the power given to those who have expertise in a certain field.

To understand expert power, think about how important the audio-visual technican is at an event. You wouldn't be able to run your event well without them, and that means they hold power over you in terms of how well your event is run and one aspect of the quality of the event.

Referent power

Referent power is the power that comes from a leader's strong relationship skills.

Referent power is very useful in situations where command and control are less acceptable, and collaboration and influence will gain greater results.

As organisations move away from traditional hierarchical leadership structures, referent power becomes more important. In other words, referent power happens when followers respect and / or admire their leaders.

To understand referent power, think about someone who you admire so much that you try to behave like them. That person has referent power over you.

Table 8.1: Type of power, adapted from Northouse (2015)

In addition to these five types of power, we can also add the following:

- **Information** power – in which power is based on the notion that one person has access to information that is important, useful – or of value – to another person.

- **Connection** power – in which power is based on the perception that someone has relationships with important or influential people.

A short note: whilst I have used Northouse's summaries of these types of power here, they are widely accepted terms throughout leadership and power literature. Readers who are interested should be able to find a wealth of writing on the intersections between power and leadership.

Access to leadership = access to power

By looking at leadership as a process of influence, scholarly research has a tendency to focus only on the positive aspects of leadership. This is a cause for concern, because it means that many ignore the negative issues around the power that leaders can hold over their followers, and the impact this power can have. Power is, after all, the ability to exercise control over others and those in leadership positions are in positions of power (both in terms of financial reward, respect and decision making). This power, derived from their position of authority, can be very beneficial and rewarding for the leaders themselves, which means they are not likely to want to relinquish this power to others. In addition, the traditional hierarchical structures that exist in most event organisations work to prevent those not in formal leadership positions from gaining access to power.

Power – or the lack thereof – may well be evident in the degree of participation of leadership and the process of leadership itself and how it can be bestowed on people, but may well exclude certain people. This of course has huge implications in terms of diversity and equality. Given the recent rise in global consciousness about these issues, questions must be asked about how much access to power those who face structural inequality in the event industry because of their gender, sexuality, or race will have.

Another concern is the lack of diversity, inclusion and representation at events themselves. In a piece of research conducted in 2020, the

Event Manger Blog looked at 150 events to determine how diverse the speaker panels really were. They found that between 35-40% of events they looked at didn't have one black speaker and, if that was widened out to include BIPOC (black, indigenous and other people of colour) and female representation, the overall picture is still really poor. This is deeply problematic, because events are platforms and many believe they have a duty of care to provide space for all, or at least a level playing field for diverse voices. And of course, there is huge value in ensuring that all areas of event communities are represented, not least because diversity means a greater richness in knowledge and experience and leads to a much more interesting event.

As I have already made clear, little is known about leadership and power within the event community – however, when we look at leadership research in general, it becomes clear that the exclusion of 'different' voices limits participation in leadership, and that power has a clear influence on relationships at work and in access to event spaces and event platforms.

The power of events and event communities

In the next few sections, we'll discuss how events can be catalysts for change – when we conceptualise events in this way, it becomes clear that the event experience itself can be a form of leadership. We can think of events as powerful in two ways. First, we can think of the event organisation's power, in terms of setting the agenda, deciding on the programme for events, and amplifying key issues (such as the way Glastonbury places sustainability and recycling at the heart of its event objectives, or the drive to include a diverse speaker panel, or a focus on specific societal or cultural topics to raise awareness). Second, we can think about the power that the event communities themselves have – the power of people coming together to bring about change. Both of these types of power are examples of leadership – the power of events therefore lies in their ability to lead change.

Crucially, as Rojek (2013) suggests, we must remember that events are not normally spontaneous expressions of people power – they are well organised, often with motivations to persuade or even to manipulate the market place. The ownership of events rarely rests with the people, and whilst events might involve parts of society joining together to celebrate (e.g. the opening ceremony of the Olympic games) or to do good (e.g. the 2020 One World: Together at Home concert or Live Aid in the 80s), they are still underpinned by a hierarchical structure that is often designed to keep the people in their place.

In addition, events have become displays of social or cultural capital (terms coined by Bourdieu). Social and cultural capital is made up of an individual's social assets – the skills, education, norms and behaviours that are acquired by a social group, and which give them economic and social advantages. Events are an excellent way for individuals to display these advantages – whether by bringing people together to celebrate the successes of a country's athletics team, or putting on a concert to raise awareness of a particular issue, people are often tempted to display their attendance at events as badges of honour, and as examples of their advantages in society.

Rojek concludes that humans habitually feel powerless and impotent in the face of the world's problems, and that events enable us to feel we are making a difference – ultimately, they enable attendees to feel good about their own responses and the infuse people with hope. As he says – *"When we see a gay rights float at the Sydney Mardi Gras, or a costume parade featuring the* pessoas humilde *(humble people) at the Rio Carnival, or the image of starving African infants broadcast on the video screen of a concert to relive hunger, we become part of an irresistible wave of global unity."* This beacon of hope makes events a seductive vehicle for a wide range of issues, from fixing the corporate culture, to raising money, to support those suffering from famine in Africa. There is power in community – though Rojek suggests that the power to do good is undone by 'magical thinking' in which people believe that just by feeling good at an event, they are doing good. And this results in no actual changes to society or any of the structural changes required to really fix the issues these events make visible.

Rojek has a rather challenging view of events – much of what he writes about the darker side of event power and the questions he asks about who runs events and why, will ring true for many readers; certainly it should be explored further. But events do also have the power to do good and they have a role to play in society – they have the power to bring people together, create and consolidate communities, generate vast sums of money for good causes, and they can raise issues to the global consciousness.

Indeed, setting objectives is the number one priority for event creators – and more and more frequently, those objectives go beyond 'making money' and look to create long term legacies – these events can be seen to be using their power of influence, and their reach, to lead on social or cultural change. Some events now put delivering long term, profound differences at the heart of what they do; others are simply taken over by protests that shift perceptions and raise awareness of societal problems.

And an example of the later is the #metoo movement, and the way it was brought to global consciousness not just through social media, but through visible protests at events like the 2018 Golden Globes Awards ceremony, where most guests dressed in black to show solidarity with the movement, and prominent actors mentioned it in their speeches.

Examples of events that display leadership regarding radical social or cultural change, and use the power of their reach to bring about real difference include the Black Lives Matters Protests – a human rights campaign that began on social media in 2013, and was highlighted during 2018 when some American sports stars began to 'take the knee' during the national anthems at sports games, particularly in the NFL. The campaign was launched into the global consciousness by the deaths of George Floyd, Ahmaud Arbery and Breonna Taylor in 2020 and the subsequent organised, and spontaneous, rallies and protests, around the world. Other obvious examples are the Rock against Racism concert in the 1970s, the Live Aid concert in 1985 and the One Love Manchester benefit concert in 2017.

It is important to note, however, that most events that have social responsibility or driving change as a core objective don't make international news. Many small-scale local events are created specifically to share knowledge, build communities and bring about change – examples include events that raise money to provide much needed equipment or buildings for the local community, or events that enable neighbours to share and learn about different cultural heritages. The power of these small local events to make significant differences to people's lives should not be diminished, just because the number of people they impact is low.

So, events can become platforms for key issues and they have the power to amplify voices that are frequently not heard. This then is one of the most important powers of events – events as social change agents. This concept is discussed in more detail in Chapter 9.

Stakeholder management, leadership and power

One final part of the power/influence puzzle in the event industry is the fact that events do not happen in a silo; in fact they are the result of a large network of stakeholders, all contributing to the event, or involved in the event, to a varying degree. Competing and sometimes conflicting organisational objectives from the various stakeholders can often result in issues with resolution and, of course, with power (Tiew et al., 2015).

This is particularly true of event organisations that are reliant on external clients or sponsors as key stakeholders and who therefore hold significant legitimate and coercive power over the relationship. When clients or sponsors are the main financial contributors to an event, then their business is essential and their ability to influence the organisation's output is therefore high (Tiew et al., 2015). Put simply, these key stakeholders hold the majority of the power in the relationship with event organisations, and as the working climate changes and pressures and priorities increase, stakeholders relay these pressures to the event team – sometimes incoherently and inconveniently. An example of this is that, over the last few years, budgets have been reduced and expectations for premium experiences delivered quickly and professionally have increased (Eventbrite, 2019) – clearly this creates significantly different pressures on the event organisations and the teams that work within them.

In addition, those stakeholders with legitimate power over the event – think here of the police, or the licensing authorities – must be managed carefully so that they do not use their power to disrupt your event planning. The same can be said for those stakeholders who can influence your event, but aren't really interested in it being a success – think here of the coercive power of the media, or the disruptive power of local communities if they resent you running your event in their space. These stakeholders can create negative PR and make running your event very difficult. Lastly, we shouldn't forget the power that our supplier stakeholders have over the event organisations – they have the power to ruin an event by supplying a poor-quality service, or not delivering the required goods in a timely fashion. Whilst the event organiser might ultimately have power over the suppliers (in that they can refuse payment and not work with them again), the suppliers pose a risk because we often don't know that they will let us down until it's too late to do anything about it!

Managing these diverse groups of stakeholders and their associated power is a form of leadership – keeping them informed and ensuring they have all the information they need is how you lead them to support your event. For a comprehensive insight into the power of stakeholders, readers should seek out *Event Stakeholders* by Niekerk and Getz (2019).

Summary

In this chapter we have explored the intersection between power and leadership, and we have seen how power is the ability to exert control over others, whereas leadership should be about the ability to influence others, without having to resort to power. That said, leadership does often need power and we have looked at the types of power that exist and how they work within leadership situations.

We have also explored the darker side of leadership and power, and have raised some key points that the event industry needs to address about access to power, and the power that events and event communities have to lead change in our society. During this discussion, I have shone a light on the wealth of things we need to know about leadership, power and events. Particularly within event organisations, academic scholars have yet to explore the key questions of 'who leads and when'. There are then questions we cannot answer about who actively, and regularly, participates in leadership when running events, and who is – or isn't – excluded from event communities. Understanding the types of power you might encounter in the events is one more step along the ladder of understanding and improving this ever changing, dynamic and hugely creative and innovative industry. I hope our readers have found this chapter useful in considering some of the key issues surrounding leadership, and have grown in confidence in understanding who leads, how they do it and what it means for those who follow.

Leadership in action: Industry insight from Carrie Abernathy

Carrie Abernathy CMP, CEM, CSEP is a 15-year events industry veteran and a blogger, speaker, coach and industry leader. Carrie co-founded the Association for Women in Events in 2015 and runs the blog: A Woman With Drive – a nod to her love of golf and leadership. Carrie is also a full-time meeting planner with Altria Group Distribution Company. She has been named a Top 25 Industry Influencer by Successful Meetings *magazine and was nominated for Meeting Planner of the Year by PCMA. She was inducted into the Smart Meetings Magazine's Smart Women Hall of Fame. Carrie resides mostly in Radford, Virginia with her dog, Ginger. She writes here on the resilience you need to be an event manager, and being a woman in the event industry.*

For more information, please visit: www.awomanwithdrive.com

I believe that being a good leader of events starts with organization and being an excellent project manager. To be a good leader of people, I believe you have to hone different skills entirely. For event management, you have to have a keen sense of time management, and the ability to see the 'bigger picture' even while the work is in progress. To be a 'good' leader, you have to have a few key traits. Empathy—to understand what your attendees are going through, what challenges your venue or vendors may have, what your stakeholders and staff need. The planners that I've worked with who display the best event leadership skills are the ones that work well under pressure and complete chaos. They prepare for the worst scenario, but they show up and are willing to actively handle all situations that may happen during their event with outward grace and composure and patience. *Great* event planners know that even though we strive for perfection, something will ultimately *not* go the way we planned and will be flexible and adjust quickly. Event planners are the ultimate catalyst for change because we have to deal with it on a daily basis.

I once heard that if event planners ran the government, we'd have no debt and the work would be finished in half the time. Although I laughed, I believe the sentiment is true. Event planners are resilient. Event planners are somehow extremely analytical, strategic, and tactical at the same time. Event planners are normally the only job in the company outside of the CEO were *everyone* touches, sees, and reviews their work. The event planning job is a very high stress one for a reason. At the most basic level, our job is to make *everyone* happy. Event planner personality skills that are most beneficial in my opinion are empathy, grace, patience, the ability to influence others. They need to be able to make fast and frank decisions and stick to a plan even through adversity and constant challenges. They need to be a clear voice of reason and lead through chaotic times.

One final thought – on being a woman in the event industry

Being a woman in the events industry is a challenge for several reason. Prior to the development of the Association for Women in Events, women only made up approximately 3-5% of C Suite level position in the industry overall, even though the industry itself was comprised of 75% women workers. The industry is only considered male dominated at the top levels. Leadership in suppliers, third party events organizations, and organizations that planners works for were mostly white males. The organization (AWE) was formed with the idea of challenging this disparity. After the organization was formed in 2015, other organizations pushed their women-centric programs forward with greater gusto. It was incredible to see the support for these new initiatives in the events industry. I believe women started to question why they weren't holding these leadership positions during that time. I feel there has been a shift, and more women are holding leadership positions, although the disparity still exists. There are definitely *more* resources now for women and women leaders in the events industry, but we still have a long way to go when it comes to leadership and boardroom representation.

Study questions

1 Thinking over your own experiences, can you find examples of when you have experienced the five different types of power, as identified in the table in this chapter?

2 This chapter proposes that some events are so powerful that they can lead change in society. Do you agree?

3 Rojek seems to suggest that attendees at events actually make little difference, and that there is a difference between feeling good and doing good. Do you think that large scale benefit events like the One Love Manchester concert, or the Together at Home online concert actually did any good? If so, outline what differences you think they made and if not, explain why you hold this view.

4 Do some research on the Live Aid concert of 1985. Can you find evidence that this event was a leader in promoting change regarding the political responses to famine in Africa?

5 The Race for Life fundraising events organised by Cancer Research UK are among the largest fundraising events in the UK. Explain what you think the power and impact of these events might be.

6 Discuss this viewpoint: Rojek suggests that events are never displays of people power, and that audiences are always being manipulated by those that fund and organise them.

7 Can you name any events that you have attended that have had a powerful impact on you? Write a list of the events you attended, and the impact they had on you personally.

8 Reflecting on the leadership in action section, do you think there is an issue with gender and power in events?

Further reading

This aspect of leadership ties in with two other books in this series:

Nieker, M.V. & Getz, D. (2019) *Event Stakeholders*. Oxford: Goodfellow Publishers http://dx.doi.org/10.23912/9781911396635-3840.

Antchak, V., Vassilios, Z and Getz, D. (2019) *Event Portfolio Management*. Oxford: Goodfellow Publishers.

Event Manager Blog. (2019) The Power of Events. Available at https://www.eventmanagerblog.com/power-of-events

Rojek, C. (2013) *Event Power: How global events manage and manipulate*. Sage Publications Ltd

References

Alvesson, M. & A. Spicer (2012). Critical leadership studies: the case for critical performativity. *Human Relations,* **65**(3), 367-390.

Bladen, C., Kennell, J., Abson, E. & Wilde, N. (2018). *Events Management: an introduction*. Oxon, Routledge.

Bolden, R. (2011). Distributed leadership in organizations: a review of theory and research. *International Journal of Management Reviews,* **13**(3), 251-269.

Bowdin, G. , Allen, J., O'Toole, W., Harris, R. & McDonnell, I. (2011). *Events Management*. London, Butterworth Heinemann.

Day, D. V., Gronn, P. & Salas, E. (2004). Leadership capacity in teams. *The Leadership Quarterly,* **15**(6), 857-880.

Ensley, M. D., Hmieleski, K.M. & Pearce, C.L. (2006). The importance of vertical and shared leadership within new venture top management teams: Implications for the performance of startups. *Leadership Quarterly,* **17**(3), 217-231.

Eventbrite (2019). 2019 Event Statistics and what they mean for your events. from https://www.eventbrite.com/blog/event-statistics-ds00/.

Event Manager Blog (2020) Diversity and Inclusion. Available at: https://www.eventmanagerblog.com/diversity-and-inclusion/.

Northouse, P. 2015. *Leadership : Theory and practice* (7th ed.) Sage.

Pernecky, T. (2015). Sustainable Leadership in Event Management. *Event Management* 19(1): 109-121.

Pine, B. J. & Gilmore, J. H. (1999). *The Experience Economy: Work is theatre and every business a stage*. Boston: Harvard Business School Press.

Rojek, C.(2013) *Event Power: How global events manage and manipulate*. Sage.

Tiew, F., et al. (2015). Tourism events and the nature of stakeholder power. *Event Management,* **19**(4), 525-541.

Van der Wagen, L. (2006). *Human Resource Management for Events : Managing the event workforce*. Oxford: Butterworth-Heinemann.

9 Modelling events as social agents of change

Dr Miriam Firth

Chapter aims

- ☐ Define social agents of change,
- ☐ Understand how events produce a stage of information and education to lead and inform society,
- ☐ Analyse how events mirror societal attitudes and behaviours,
- ☐ Explore motivations and outcomes for leaderless events,
- ☐ Identify how economies driving events management lead to new employment practices.
- ☐ Focus on leadership in action: Industry insight from Rose Wilcox of The Leadmill on music venues as social agents of change.

Introduction

This chapter offers a model of events as social agents of change to outline how leadership in, and through, events evidence leadership of societal change. First, 'social agents of change' is defined to clarify this term to apply to the model. Following this, each area of the model is discussed to identify how events can be modelled as social agents of change. Through this model, you can consider how events provide information and education, how events clarify societal behaviour and action, how leaderless events support cultural and political issues, and how events management has created new employability practices. Each element of this model refers to theory and case studies to provide support for events being seen as social agents of change. The summary offers the model in full and student questions offered at the end enable you to apply this in your studies to complete critical analysis of events as social agents of change.

Social agents of change: A definition

A social agent of change (SAC) can be a person, group or outcome from a range of activities. They are signalled as the start, or leader, in changing existing phenomena. Social agents of change as a term is rooted in Sociology theory, as they evidence a change in existing social practices, scaled according to the issue actioned. Although the origins of the term have been linked to university students in Canada in the 1960s (see Lemon, 2004), in contemporary practice SACs can be seen in businesses and individuals.

An excellent example of organisations set up to change existing phenomena is 'Grind out Hunger'. This is a not for profit organisation whose mission is to empower youth to take leadership in the fight against childhood hunger and malnutrition, through their passions of skateboarding, surfing, snowboarding and music. The following table offers case examples of both businesses and individuals who could be seen as SACs:

Businesses	Individuals
Grind Out Hunger (www.facebook.com/grindouthunger/)	Maria Shriver
Impakt (https://www.impaktcorp.com/)	Teachers
Ford Motor Company fighting HIV/Aids in South Africa	Emma Gonzalez
Green Mountain Coffee fair trade deals	Shamma bint Suhail Faris Mazrui

Table 9.1: Social agents of change: businesses and individuals

The examples offered in the table above evidence how SACs are not always one action or person but can be a combined effort by groups of people to change societal issues. An SAC is not always created to lead in societal change though. Film and media, for example, can serve to question the status quo in society to enable viewers to consider ways in which society act and behave (Bapis, 2014). Other examples of SAC use is noted in linguistics (Charity, 2008), mobile phone use (Nurallah, 2009) and migrant participation in society (Burgess, 2004; Grabowska et al. 2016)., Therefore, although SACs are noted as a singular term, they are present in a wide range of businesses, individuals, media production, communication forms and members of society. If you raised money for a charity, you are also an SAC as you are raising awareness of the charity and signalling support is required for the charity's cause.

In terms of the governance and form of an SAC, this can also vary. SACs can be created as profitable or not-for-profit. They can also be private, public or volunteer managed. In terms of the profit framework for an SAC, if the issue or cause requires fundraising for others then it could be a charitable event or sequence of events to raise money. However, if new products are used to raise the money, then there may be profits required in the fair payment of people working within or to support the SAC. So, for example, an SAC may be set up as non-for-profit and then later require profit according to the activities needed to grow and increase the impact of their efforts. In terms of the public/private/ volunteer nature of SACs this will also depend on the issue or cause. There are a number of non-government organisations (NGOs) considered SACs (Pearce,1993). This is perhaps an obvious link as NGOs are created by citizens and usually have humanitarian aims or objectives. You may expect an SAC to be an NGO, but examples in this chapter offer a range of private, public and volunteer organisations which are considered SACs. Also, if an NGO does not lead to social change it cannot be defined as an SAC. For example, if Oxfam supports a local community in building new schools, but does not change local practice or political support, they cannot be seen as an SAC in that particular context and situation.

From this discussion, it is evident that SACs are present throughout global society. Even if they are not labelled, or marketed, as an SAC, countless people and organisations desire to challenge, address and improve social issues. The industry, form and structure of the SAC could be emergent rather than designed. The issue is often immediately addressed by citizen action which is then later formalised into an organisation acting for social change.

Issues SACs champion, support or challenge

When in progress an SAC will raise awareness of key issues linked or included in the phenomena to be changed. This section seeks to outline some of the issues contemporary SACs have addressed. SACs will champion, support or challenge existing perceived societal issues to support social change. Some of the common issues addressed by SACs include climate change, sustainability, gender equality, racial equality, healthcare issues, fair trade and inclusion. The issues may be specific geographic scales also: local, regional, national or international. The change does not have to be global to have an effect and the issue it champions can relate to a small area or group of people.

Probably the most widely known global issue championed by SACs is that of climate change and the sustainability of our planet. This is a known issue across the world and has been highlighted most recently by the work of Greta Thunberg (a clear SAC). Greta's medical history coupled with her environmental activism is a story which has had a global impact. From school strikes to protests, her activism work has increased discussion on climate issues in many world nations. This is an interesting example of an SAC as the issue is not new, but through the SAC the issue has been brought to the public's attention and enabled wider debate and consideration of the ways to reduce our impact on the natural environment.

Within climate change activism there is, on the surface at least, a seemingly odd suggestion by the United Nations: that women should be *the* people tackling the issue (UN, 2020). This position is established as it is recognised that climate change may affect women and girls the most:

"especially women and girls, who bear the brunt" (UN, 2020)

This suggestion is supported through positioning women as leaders in most agricultural sectors in rural or poor areas in the world. Farming is most affected by climate change as the usual seasons in the year are changing due to temperamental weather patterns. This impacts agricultural sectors in rural and poorer economic locations as they lack the funding for technology to work around the shifts in weather patterns. Focussing on female leadership as an SAC here is particularly interesting as it is directly contradicts the usual gender inequality seen: traditionally men are favoured for senior leadership positions.

The Black Lives Matter movement is an SAC challenging racially motivated violence in society. Starting in 2012 after the death of Trayvon Martin in Sanford, USA, it has had continued success in raising awareness of racial profiling and violence due to racial profiling. This movement is particularly interesting as the issue is, in most countries, an illegal one. Violence against anyone is illegal, but violence due to prejudice or racial profiling is also considered direct discrimination (Citizens Advice, 2020). After 2012, the movement has continued but most notably been active in 2020 after the police killed George Floyd in Minneapolis, USA. In 2020 there were marches and protests across the world supporting the movement and millions of social media posts trended with the hashtag #blacklivesmatter. This global awareness also led to the creation of further SACs: White Lives Matter, All Lives Matter and Blue Lives Matter. All of these linked SACs challenge profiling a person due to their race, ethnicity or profession. The core of the message is that there is violence in society due to racial profiling and this needs to stop.

The discussion in this section has focussed on social activism SACs which focus on the issues of climate change and racial profiling. This is not all encompassing of the issues linked to SACs but offer some depth to case studies on SAC issues. Some more examples of SACs and their associated issues are offered below, to research and consider.

SAC	Issue addressed
Netherlands Alzheimer Cafes (Cels et al. 2012)	Social spaces were needed for families to discuss and support patients with Alzheimer's disease.
Me to We www.metowe.com/	Social enterprise offering volunteer tourism and fair trade retail. (issues noted in Volunteer Tourism see Ooi & Laing 2010).
Good Lad Initiative - Dan Guinness www.goodladinitiative.com/	Challenging rigid male stereotypes in the UK to support gender equality in the community.
Grameen Bank www.grameen.com/	Banking which is usually unavailable to residents in Bangladesh is supported by this bank who uses appropriate lending criteria based on trust to support the poorest in society.

Table 9.2: SACs and Issues they have addressed

This section has outlined some the societal issues addressed by case studies of contemporary SACs. As these address issues and changes needed in society they are often emergent rather than pre-designed through a profitable business plan. This is an important element in SACs: they require traction, community and action in order to be perceived as successful.

Events as SACs

In terms of understanding or positioning events as SACs, this is a relatively new, and sometimes contested link. Historically events are seen to be created through the heritage of local traditions and celebrations which have then led to larger scale profitable event businesses. St Patrick's Day and Notting Hill Carnival are two such examples of when a local tradition grows to become a significant economic contributor both locally and internationally. However, from discussion in this chapter it is clear that almost every SAC will require events in order to gather people together to discuss and raise awareness of the issues and changes they want within the society. It is, therefore, clear that SACs depend upon events to ensure citizens can actively participate in understanding the issues at hand. Modelling all events as SACs is a nuanced shift from this though. SACs using events is different to seeing all events as SACs. There is also a body of literature on the social impacts of events (see Richards et al., 2013 for example) but this, again, is not the focus or position this chapter offers. This section offers discussion on existing published literature on the links between events, events management and SACs. This will offer a basis from which the model of events as SACs will be drawn from.

To begin, if you were to search "event/s management" and "social agents of change" you would find there is no body of literature publishing research linking these two areas of theory in contemporary English publications. Instead, the links are made between events management and agents of social change for which there are less than 100 publications available and less than 10 of these explicitly analyse SACs and events management. From another field of study, sociology, there is also little published and linked between sociology and events management as SACs. This finding, or a lack of findings, is interesting as SACs require movements of people to come together in events in order to thrive and raise awareness of or create social change.

To begin discussion of existing positions on events linked to SACs it is interesting to find that the earliest mention of SACs linked to events management and its associated fields of study is that of Butler (1975). Butler (1975) analysed a model for tourism outlining how tourism created a place, or stage, for people to gather and learn about cultural differences. The need for cultural empathy and understanding in society has been a consistent demand since the wars of the 20th century and the subsequent globalisation of the world via access to travel. By travelling and meeting others, tourists are seen as being within an SAC which supports global awareness and intercultural competence. The destination they arrive in is the platform, or stage from which they view, interact and understand other cultures. Events can also be seen as a stage for SACs as people who attend will learn about social issues which require change (Ong & Goh, 2018).

Events in museums are seen as SACs as they mirror society and local history offering information and raising awareness on historic events (Chhabra, 2009). School education through museum exhibitions is also seen as an SAC vital for local history education (Redaelli, 2019). These papers offer confirmation that arts events in museums are natural SACs as they educate and reflect upon society's history. The form of change created is often through education and knowledge development, but this can also lead to societal change from awareness raising. For example, visiting the National Holocaust Centre and Museum in Newark, UK would inform you of how prejudice and racial profiling led to mass genocide. The aim of the museum is not to promote genocide, but to *"encourage personal responsibility and the promotion of fairness and justice"* (Smith, 2020). Therefore, visitors of this museum would not only learn about the history of the Holocaust, but be actively encouraged to be more socially responsible and act fairly towards others.

Sharpe (2007) identified how small scale music festivals can be SACs through mixing music with political agendas and ideas. For any avid festival attendee the political link is well known and seen. Festivals enable gatherings of large groups of people to share, experience and learn from each other and political groups are often seen within these promoting and sharing their policies and agendas with the public in attendance. SACs using events for political issues are also often seen in marches, protests or movements. The protests against #blacklivesmatter marches and Greta's school strikes are two such examples already noted in this chapter. Sharpe's (2007) discussion of a political music festival is interesting and can certainly confirm an event as an SAC. More often though events are used as SACs in leaderless events for protests, marches or strikes.

Discussing some of the (very) limited literature linking events and events management to SACs is it clear that they can provide a stage for social learning and change, they can mirror society leading to socially responsible action, and can challenge political ideals in leaderless events. Before moving to outline the model presented in this chapter it is important to outline sociology's perspective on this.

Horne and Manzenreiter (2006) noted that the perception of events being linked to societal impact and change is:

"seen as something as a joke by mainstream sociology until recently"(p.1)

This article suggests that in the sports events management research and literature, sociology has not been linked thoroughly to the impacts and outcomes of sporting events. There is a large body of literature on the legacy and impact of sporting events and there is a missing link to how these influence society change as they can be seen as SACs. Rojek (2014) later confirms this position in noting that events have not established effective links between events management and Sociology theory to effectively clarify how events can operate as SACs and support societal issues. Therefore, although SACs are well established across the world, the link to how events can be perceived a leading in societal change is relatively under-represented in existing published research.

With a lack of published literature available to consider events as SACs, this chapter seeks to fill a perceived gap in knowledge by offering a new model of events as social agents of change. The model created is split into four parts: events as stages, events as mirrors of society, leaderless events and events leading to new employment practice. The first three are evidently drawn from the discussion above, but the fourth is from my own experience in managing and running events. The four areas are offered as a new conceptual framework to position events as SACs and critically analyse how events could be viewed as SACs.

Events are a stage

Earlier discussion on events as SACs outlined how an event can be seen as a stage to present or address issues to event attendees. Whether this is cultural awareness (as a tourist) or learning about political agendas (at music and politics festivals), event attendees are presented with information and experiences which can lead to changes in society. For example, the 'One World, Together at Home' event of 2020/1 was a music event which praised the work of healthcare professionals working through the COVID19 pandemic, whilst educating the attendees to act as 'Global Citizens' and complete 15 actions to support stopping the spread of the virus. This event was requested by the United Nations (UN) and World Health Organisation (WHO) so that attendees could both celebrate through music and actively support the public during a global pandemic. Attendees were not required to visit a venue, but were actively encouraged to stay at home and enjoy music from leading artists across the world. Similar to the 'Live Aid' concert of 1985 the 'One World: Together at Home' event is an SAC to support contemporary society issues.

To further explore this part of the model two aspects are discussed: events as thought leaders, and education and training through events.

Events as thought leaders

A thought leader is a business or someone who is recognised as a leading expert on a particular subject. The following table notes case examples of events which are both thought leaders and SACs to aid leading change in society.

Title	Attendees	Event type	SAC issue addressed
Web Summit websummit.com/	+100,000	Conference	Female leaders in the technology industry. Equality in employment practice. Societal issues linked to Technology development.
Summit summit.co/	+1500	Conference	Brings together experts from society to create ideas and initiatives to solve societal issues.
Ted Talks www.ted.com/talks	Millions	Conference	Spreading ideas and information on important societal topics.

Table 9.3: Thought leader events

Education & training through events

Events are often created with the primary purpose of educating and training attendees. Education and training events enable attendees to develop knowledge in particular areas, but some events result in education due to the topic/s in which they are focussed. A few examples are noted below:

Title	Attendees	Event type	SAC issue addressed
Koningsdag	+800,000	Festival	Education on the history of the royal family in the Netherlands
Pride Festivals	Millions worldwide	Festival	Educating and celebrating lesbian, gay, bisexual, and transgender people.
BETT Show www.bettshow.com	+30,000	Trade Show	Transforming education technology to support future educational practices.
LEEF www.leef.org.uk	+800 followers	Forum	A London based educators' forum which hosts annual conferences on urban environmental issues.

Table 9.4: Events which educate on societal issues

Looking at the examples of events offered in the above two tables it is clear that these fall into the Meetings, Incentives, Conferences and Exhibitions (MICE) category, or typology, of events (Shone & Parry, 2004). This is interesting as the opening case example of two music events are different to these. If you thought of a stage in an event you may naturally think of a theatre, or music venue stage. By offering examples from the MICE sector the cases in this section have outlined how for-profit and non-staged events can also be seen as SACs. They do not need a stage to publicise, inform and engage attendees into action. The event itself *is* the stage.

Events are also seen as a public stage as they can involve whole societies (e.g. Pride and Koningsdag). These events are noted as SACs as they can be linked to sociology theorist accounts of action:

"*Ritualized, civic, events and ceremonies (Durkheim); rationalized, bureaucratically organized, science driven behaviour (Weber); commercial, global spectacles (Marx); expressivity and the everyday (Simmel and postmodernism); and male cultural displays and cultural centres (feminism).*" (Horne & Manzenreiter, 2006: p.1)

The above quotation confirms that social action and activity is rooted in the production of community events and can lead to educating the attendees on social history, action and behaviour. In this way, events can be seen as a stage which produces information to inform, challenge and develop societal norms.

Events are mirrors of society

Events were traditionally created to support local and personal celebrations around societal frameworks (such as birthdays or marriages). National holiday celebrations are also present in most countries whereby historic events are remembered (such as Thanksgiving). As such, events are created, accessed and attended by most communities across the world. With this background to events management, it is noted that events can be seen as miniature communities, or Petri dishes, of society from which you can analyse human behaviour. In conjunction, events can also lead to societal changes in behaviour if they educate and require different behaviours. SAC are notable when event attendee behaviour is undesirable and later action seeks to alter this, and also event engagement leads to changes in attendee behaviour after the event. Poor behaviour and promotion of new behaviours through events are now discussed to evidence how events as mirrors of society can lead to social change.

Poor human behaviour

This position is most notable within festival attendee behaviour and the disposal of waste and possessions on site. From a 3-year on-site study completed at the UK's Glastonbury Festival to support their 'Love the Farm, Leave no Trace' campaign (Glastonbury Festivals, 2020) management sought to correct poor attendee behaviour concerning waste management. This campaign was created to support the reduction of waste and the overall negative impact of attendee behaviour on the festival site. With over 200,000 attendees, this festival is a mega-event which produces a mega amount of waste. When completing exit surveys with attendees at this festival in 2015 several people were noting that they had taken their tent and possessions away and not littered, and yet they were not carrying anything on their departure. They knew that they should not litter, reported this in the survey, and yet did not act or behave in a way which represented this. It was clear they had a social conscience on appropriate behaviour and treating the site correctly, but for whatever reason, they did not all act in the appropriate way when on site. This position is confirmed in Musgrave and Henderson's publications, and they note that understanding on- and off-site attendee behaviour is important to ensure events are sustainable and attendees treat their local environments appropriately at all times (Musgrave, 2011; Henderson & Musgrave, 2014; Musgrave & Henderson, 2015).

The example of the Glastonbury festival offered above links to publications around escapism and hedonism sought by event attendees. Poor attendee behaviour can be linked to this as the attendees choose to act in socially unacceptable ways even though in external societies they act appropriately. Event attendees do not always want to behave in the same socially appropriate way, but instead, seek hedonistic pleasures whilst attending events (Getz & Page, 2016). This clarifies how attendee motivations can lead to poor attendee behaviour, but also shines a light on a society's needs for escapism via hedonistic actions (Stebbins, 2001). The human need for escapism is most notable in computer games, like World of Warcraft (Kuo et al., 2016), whereby people choose to play games where they are creating new characters for themselves.

Pilcher and Eade's (2016) research is of note here as they identify categories of festival attendee motivations and behaviour based around demographic analysis. Their five categories of attendees clarify how the local community of a folk festival behaves according to their grouped demographic status. Therefore, attendee demographics can be suggested as a reason for poor attendee behaviour. In my research completed at Glastonbury, the majority of attendees were attending for the first time and below the age of 25. They noted that they did not want to clean up their area of camping due to the high ticket price and that they felt others should clean up after them. Finally, when considering sporting events, Aicher et al. (2015) confirmed that attendees all behave and act in similar ways, regardless of their tourist or resident demographic status. This section confirms that although societal norms are present and acknowledged, event attendees can sometimes act contrary to these due to the cost of the event and their desire to seek hedonistic, escapist experiences. In this way event attendees are social agents of change going against societal norms in order to experience and enjoy events. This can have negative consequences for event managers and increase the negative environmental impacts of events.

Promotion of new human behaviours

Event campaigns and new event concepts can lead to changes in attendee behaviours during and after events. The Love the Farm, Leave no Trace campaign at the Glastonbury festival has raised awareness of attendee behaviour and has led to an increase in reusing materials, reducing waste and respecting the local environment (Glastonbury Festivals, 2020). Strafford et al. (2018) noted how pop-up shopping centre events create enlivenments and add to the usual shopping experiences. Instead of solely completing shopping and eating activities in a shopping centre, or mall, customers can immerse themselves in additional events which can lengthen their commercial experiences. Product displays, food samples, demonstrations, and leafleting local causes are all examples of how these retail events can lead to altered human behaviours. The Affordable Art Fair in Singapore offers an event where more people have access and opportunity to purchase art, as this is seen as too expensive for the majority of the local population. Educational events will also lead to altered attendee behaviours as they will gain knowledge to consider alternative ways of acting and behaving.

This section has discussed how events can mirror societal human action and behaviour. Issues of escapism and hedonism have been noted as barriers to positive attendee behaviour, and campaigns and event concepts clarify how events can lead to positive social change due to issues seen in society.

Events can be leaderless

The previous two sections have noted how event concepts can be seen as SAC and how altering attendee behaviour in events can lead to SAC. This section will now outline how leaderless events contribute to perceiving events as SAC. This is based upon Rojek's (2014) paper which outlines how some events can be viewed as leaderless. Leaderless events are:

> *"forms of collective mobilization and direct action that are externally constituted without a leader."* (Rojek, 2014: p.352)

This term suggests that when an event is created and led by a society's needs, rather than a small group of individuals or businesses objectives, it can create mobilised groups of society to act and challenge societal issues. Whether or not there is a single leader in these events is contested. In essence, they are created due to a spontaneous societal problem perceived with the state, government, or society. As such, these events are usually seen in the form of protests, movements or demonstrations. Examples of historical leaderless events are noted below with comments on how they attribute to the model on SACs.

Gandhi's Salt March (India, the 1930s)

This demonstration of civil disobedience required thousands of activists across India acting against national laws. They demanded sovereign rule from the British and that the British rule in India was only due to the consent of Indian communities. Although this event did not lead to an immediate change in Indian rule, the campaign and marches enabled Indian people to confirm their civil rights requirements in solidarity across a nation.

South Africa's National Day of Protest (1950)

On 26th June 1950 over 500 delegates and 10,000 people attended events to protest the Suppression of Communism Bill in South Africa. This event and rally was part of a building series of protests called the Defiance Campaign based in South Africa. This campaign was tackling apartheid laws which sought to segregate citizens according to their race.

The March on Washington (USA, 1963)

This march was to protest and demand civic and economic rights for African Americans living in America. The march only lasted 3 hours, but it was preceded by years of meetings to establish clear demands in the political and economic change needed. Over 250,000 people attended the march and it resulted in pressuring the administration into a new civil rights bill in congress.

Gandi (India), Nelson Mandela (South Africa) and Martin Luther King (Washington) are famous figures involved in the above examples of leaderless events. Although they are linked and signalled as important leaders within the movements, they were not the leaders of the events. They aided in creating a national movement against existing political restrictions within the countries and resulted in positive outcomes for citizens living in the countries. A further example of contemporary leaderless events are the Brexit marches and protests completed across the United Kingdom. It will take some years to note how these affect political change, but they too signal social unrest in political change.

Events lead to new employment practices

Events are often noted for their positive economic impact (Van Winkle et al. 2016; Getz & Page 2016). Since their significant growth in western economies in the last 50 years events are seen as a core form of tourism and leisure activity supporting Gross National Outputs. Winning contracts to produce major sporting events, like the Olympics, or being the host to world-leading events, leads to increased skills and knowledge production within a society (Department for Business, Innovation & Skills, 2009). In tandem with the growth of the events industry, it is clear that new employment practices are emerging. Employment practices are said to need alteration to support environmental concerns (Musgrave, 2008) but there is evidence that the growth in events has led to altered and improved employment practices.

Company	Employment practice
Clearwater Events clearwaterevents.co.uk/	Uses a sustainable and equality led strategy to deliver events to all communities.
Ethical Staffing https://ethicalstaff.co.uk My Cause UK mycauseuk.com/	Employment and volunteering positions in events through the promotion of equal and fair employment practices.
Event Well Ltd https://eventwell.org/	Campaigning for better mental health and wellbeing in the events industry
Bearded Kitten beardedkitten.com/	Employs a 'kaleidoscope' of staff. Supports equality and fair employment practices.

Table 9.5: Event management companies and their employment practices supporting social change

Events management often requires temporary or fixed-term contracts (Firth, 2020). As such, events employees do not complete traditional forms of contracted work, but will often have portfolio careers (defined in Greenspan, 2017). This change has not come from a perceived societal issue but is emergent due to the increase in the events sector working environments, which are often temporary and sporadic (Abson, 2017)[1].

---

1 The same can be noted in home based working as a result of the global pandemic from Covid-19. There is a resulting change in employment practice due to a shift in economic and political frames surrounding the work which may lead to altered working practices.

When reviewing the top event management companies and managers, there are common themes: innovation, creativity, socially inclusive and active social change (environmental, sustainably and employment). Table 9.1 offers examples of event management companies who deliver employment practices which can be noted as SAC.

The above examples showcase how event management companies not only exist to satisfy economic growth but support enhanced employment practice also. When operating within a temporary and patchwork field of work it is clear events have to adopt employment practices to support the health and well-being of their staff. In this way, events can lead to employment practices to meet the needs of both the industry and societal fluctuations.

Summary

This chapter has offered a model of events as social agents of change. Through the definition of social agents of change it is clear these have the power to lead change in society and improve conditions and practices. They may be individuals or businesses, but they all lead to a change in societal action and behaviour. The model presented on events as social change agents included four elements presented below:

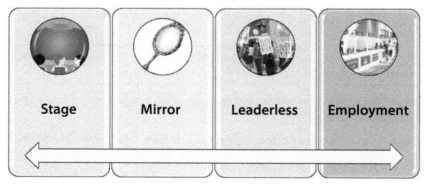

Figure 9.1: A model of events as social agents of change

Events are seen as a stage from which information is presented to raise awareness of societal issues, educate and train attendees. They can be noted as a mirror of social behaviour and seek to challenge social norms or support escapist needs. Leaderless events provide protests which challenge existing political frameworks. Finally, employment practices

9: Modelling events as social agents of change

in events management showcase emerging employment forms and ways of working to support employees across the industry. Through this chapter and presentation of the model, it is evident how events not only provide excellent leadership, but also lead societal change to improve the communities and locations in which the events are produced.

Leadership in action: Industry insight from Rose Wilcox, Commercial Manager, The Leadmill

The Leadmill is one of Sheffield's largest & oldest independent Grassroots Music Venues, boasting two separate stages with a capacity of 900 and 250.

Over the past 5 years, we have welcomed 750,505 attendees, leading to our status as Sheffield's premier live music venue. The venue has an unrivalled heritage and we are fiercely cherished by generations who have unbeatable memories of watching artists perform on both stages. We are fortunate to have won multiple awards, including Live UK's 'Best Venue Teamwork' & NME Mag 'Best Live Music Venue.'

We invest in promoting emerging artists who go on to perform at stadiums internationally – Muse, The 1975, Amy Winehouse, Coldplay and George Ezra are examples of acts that have honed their craft within our walls. Similarly, we provide supporting slots for local artists to help develop talent within our region as frequently as possible. For our team, there is a huge potential for career development – we have engineers and promoters that have garnered valuable experience working here and earning hugely successful careers within the industry. We are fortunate to work in partnership with top agencies such as CAA, WMG, Coda & ITB, as well as national promoters such as SJM & Live Nation.

Since its transformation from a disused flour mill in 1980, The Leadmill has evolved to establish itself as a multi-purpose venue with significant musical heritage and a pillar of pride in the South Yorkshire community. Sheffield displays a rich musical history of celebrated musicians that dates back to before The Leadmill's time, however, it is arguable that without venues such as ours offering their platforms to artists, their success would be limited and Sheffield's status as a musical destination would not be as illustrious as it is today.

Venues like The Leadmill are facilitators in the development of artists' live performance skills, and the promotion of events where they perform aid in growing dedicated fan bases at the early stages of their careers and beyond. Pulp in the 1980s and The Arctic Monkeys 20 years later, are both momentous examples of artists whose careers have been shaped during their time spent within The Leadmill's walls. Often we see bands beginning their career as support acts to other artists; it gives the opportunity to capture new audiences to build upon, something that both of these artists achieved.

Since its opening, The Leadmill has been building and sustaining a reputation as a venue that passionately promotes quality music of various genres, including guitar-based or Indie music, due to its popularity at the time the venue opened. It is through the deliberate and regular programming of this genre, whether at live music events or club nights, that the venue's profile and brand is developed, attracting specific communities within the region and developing an actively engaged audience that is in tune with the culture that has been created.

This profile, or brand of the venue, enables artists that perform as part of its programme to not only hone their craft within a professional, dedicated environment, but also the opportunity to speak to the venue's committed, enthusiastic and completely engaged audiences.

Their performances at The Leadmill align to become a part of the bands' own culture – references are made to Pulp and The Arctic Monkeys early events to this day, by people that loved to attend events at The Leadmill before either of the artists reached any long-term success.

Committed and interested audiences enjoying live music performances from acts like Pulp or The Arctic Monkeys, or responding to their music at club nights, naturally invites interest from music industry bodies; record labels, bookings agents and management companies actively search for popularity trends within venues in order to assist them in sourcing who they should be acquiring to develop further. Once these artists are recognised by the industry, developed and exposed on an international level, the venues that supported those initial stages of their journey are recognised as the leading force in their initial stages to success.

At The Leadmill, what began as a project to nurture undiscovered musical talent from across the world, whilst providing memorable experiences for inhabitants of the city and beyond, naturally progressed into compiling a vast range of events in order to serve various communities in the region.

Over the past 40 years, the venue has programmed substantial entertainment in many different art forms and genres, not just guitar based music, serving and welcoming over 750,000 people through its doors, attending almost 1,800 events since 2015 alone.

Inevitably, when operating with such attentiveness to your customers' interests in order to achieve a positive reputation and allow your business to grow, The Leadmill has found itself subconsciously carving the way for new trends and cultural experiences for people to enjoy. When you are assisting in the development of numerous communities' interests, providing a space for those people to explore and grow their interests, you are helping to shape the cultural landscape that you then can become such a significant part of.

By paying such close attention to the society that the venue is connected to, consistently striving to organise events that serve these varied communities that make up the fabric of its network, The Leadmill has efficiently amassed a considerable, respected presence within the region, as well as the National music and events industry. In turn, this enables the venue to speak to its own community, often behaving as influencers or contributors to people's choices in what they engage with when it comes to arts and cultural experiences.

Study questions

1 From Table 9.1, pick an example from each column and search for information on their work as an SAC. What issue are they highlighting and what are the differences in their actions to lead to change?

2 Have you ever watched a movie or TV show which has led to you questioning how society acts? Did this lead to reconsideration of your existing views on this?

3 What do you think about the UN's note on females being the leaders for climate change social agents of change? Do you agree? Discuss with others in your class.

4 Have you attend an event with the sole purpose of learning something? What did you learn and how was this applied outside of the event?

5 If events are being run more online during the pandemic, do you think this will affect attendee behaviour in events? If so, how?

6 Can you have a hedonistic festival experience in an online event? How could these elements be transformed to online events?

7 Have you ever attended a protest or march? Why did you do this and what did you intend to achieve in your attendance?

8 Do you plan to work in one company or a range of companies? If you would for a range of companies what form of career would this be called?

9 How do event management companies support emerging employment practices?

Further reading

Hayhurst, L. M. C. (2013) Girls as the 'new' agents of social change? Exploring the 'girl effect' through sport, gender and development programs in Uganda', *Sociological Research Online*, 18(2), 192–203. doi: 10.5153/sro.2959.

Roche, M. (2017). *Mega-events and Social Change : Spectacle, legacy and public culture*. Manchester: Manchester University Press.

Examples of leadership linked to societal issues and re-imagining leadership for social change: https://www.linkedin.com/pulse/8-great-books-purpose-driven-leaders-sheri-nasim/

More examples of events companies acting as SACs;

Waggle Events - https://waggleevents.org/contact/

Isla - https://weareisla.co.uk/

References

Abson, E. (2017). How event managers lead: Applying competency school theory to event management. *Event Management*, **21**(4), 403–419.

Aicher, T.J., Karadakis, K. & Eddosary, M. (2015). Comparison of sport tourists' and locals' motivation to participate in a running event. *International Journal of Event and Festival Management*, **6**(3), 215–234.

Bapis, E. (2014). *Camera and Action: American Film as Agent of Social Change, 1965-1975*. Performing Arts.

Burgess, C. (2004). (Re)constructing identities: International marriage migrants as potential agents of social change in a globalising Japan. *Asian Studies Review*, **28**, 223–242.

Butler, R. W. (1975). *Tourism as Agent of Social Change*. Presented at the International Geographic Union's Working Group on the Geography of Tourism and Recreation. Peterborough, Ontario, Canada.

Cels, S., Jong, J. & Nauta, F. (2012). *Agents of Change: Strategy and Tactics for Social Innovation*. Brookings Institution Press.

Charity, A.H. (2008). Linguists as agents for social change. *Language and Linguistics Compass*, 2(5), 923–939.

Chhabra, D. (2009) Proposing a sustainable marketing framework for heritage tourism, *Journal of Sustainable Tourism*, **17**(3), 303-320, DOI: 10.1080/09669580802495758.

Citizens Advice (2020) Discrimination because of race. https://www.citizensadvice.org.uk/law-and-courts/discrimination/discrimination-because-of-race-religion-or-belief/discrimination-because-of-race/ [Accessed on 20/02/2020].

Department for Business, Innovation & Skills (2009). *Skills for Growth: The national skills strategy*. https://www.gov.uk/government/publications/skills-for-growth-the-national-skills-strategy.

Firth, M. (2020). *Employability and Skills Handbook for Tourism, Hospitality and Events Students*. 1st ed. Abingdon: Routledge/Taylor & Francis.

Getz, D. & Page, S.J. (2016). Progress and prospects for event tourism research. *Tourism Management*, **52**, 593–631. http://dx.doi.org/10.1016/j.tourman.2015.03.007.

Glastonbury Festivals. (2020). Love the Farm, Leave no Trace. https://www.glastonburyfestivals.co.uk/information/green-glastonbury/love-the-farm-leave-no-trace/ [Accessed 06/09/2020].

Grabowska, I., Garapich, M.P., Jaźwińska, E. & Radziwinowiczówna, A. (2016). *Migrants as Agents of Change: Social Remittances in an Enlarged European Union*. Springer.

Greenspan, M. (2017). *How to Launch a Successful Portfolio Career*. https://hbr.org/2017/05/how-to-launch-a-successful-portfolio-career.

Henderson, S. & Musgrave, J. (2014). Changing audience behaviour : festival goers and throwaway tents. *International Journal of Event and Festival Management*, **5**(3), 247–262.

Horne, J. & Manzenreiter, W. (2006). An introduction to the sociology of sports mega-events. *Sociological Review*, **54**(2), 1–24.

Kuo, A., Lutz, R. & Hiler, J. (2016). Brave new World of Warcraft : a conceptual framework for active escapism. *Journal of Consumer Marketing*, **33**(7), 498–506.

Lemon, K.A. (2004). *Agent of Social Change: A history of Canadian University Press*. Ryerson University and York University.

Musgrave, J. (2011). Moving towards responsible events management. *Worldwide Hospitality and Tourism Themes*, 3(3), 258–274.

Musgrave, J. & Henderson, S. (2015). Changing audience behaviour: A pathway to sustainable event management. In Hall, M., Gossling, S., and Scott, D., *The Routledge Handbook of Tourism and Sustainability*, Routledge, p. 13.

Nurallah, A. (2009). The cell phone as an agent of social change. *Rocky Mountain Communication Review*, **6**(1), 19–25. https://ssrn.com/abstract=1482386.

Ong, F. & Goh, S., (2018) Pink is the new grey: Events as Agents of Social Change, *Event Management*, **22**, 965-979.

Ooi, N. & Laing, J.H. (2010). Backpacker tourism: sustainable and purpose-ful? Investigating the overlap between backpacker tourism and volunteer tourism motivations. *Journal of Sustainable Tourism*, **18**(2), 191–206.

Pearce, J. (1993). NGOs and Social Change: Agents or Facilitators ? *Development in Practice*, 3(3), 222–227.

Pilcher, D.R. & Eade, N. (2016). Understanding the audience: Purbeck Folk Festival. *International Journal of Event and Festival Management*, 7(1), 21–49.

Redaelli, E. (2019). *Connecting Arts and Place: Cultural Policy and American Cities*. Cham: Springer International Publishing.

Richards, G., de Brito, M. & Wilks, L. (eds) (2013), *Exploring the Social Impacts of Events*, London: Taylor & Francis Group.

Rojek, C. (2014). Leaderless organization, world historical events and their contradictions: The 'Burning Man City' case. *Cultural Sociology*, 8(3), 351–364.

Sharpe, E., (2008) Festivals and social change: Intersections of pleasure and politics at a community music festival, *Leisure Sciences*, 30(3), 217-234, DOI: 10.1080/01490400802017324

Shone, A. & Parry, B. (2004). *Successful Event Management: A practical handbook*. Cengage Learning.

Smith, J (2020) Our Story, The National Holocaust Centre and Museum, https://www.holocaust.org.uk/our-history. [Accessed 20/02/2021]

Stebbins, R.A. (2001). The costs and benefits of hedonism: some consequences of taking casual leisure seriously. *Leisure Studies*, 20(4), 305–309. DOI: 10.1080/02614360110086561.

Strafford, D., Crowther, P. & Schofield, P. (2018). Enlivenment and the Gruffalo: the unfolding story of events in destination shopping centres. *International Journal of Event and Festival Management*, 9(2), 1758–2954.

UN. (2020). Women as Agents of Social Change for Climate Change. https://www.un.org/en/climatechange/women-agents-change.shtml [Accessed 05/09/2020].

Van Winkle, C.M., Cairns, A., MacKay, K. & Halpenny, E.A. (2016). Mobile device use at festivals: Opportunities for value creation. *International Journal of Event and Festival Management*, 7(3), 201–218.

Index

authentic leadership (*see also* ethical leadership) 5, 65, 68-70

authoritarian leadership (see also Theory X and Y) 34-35

behaviours / behavioural leadership (see also path-goal theory) 8, 26-30, 32

charismatic leadership (*see also* ethical leadership; heroic leadership) 5, 45-47, 50, 59, 66

classic approaches, of leadership (*see also* entity approaches, behavioural theories, contingency theories, Theory X and Y) 23-36

coercive power (*see also* legitimate power, reward power, expert power, referent power) 140, 145

collective leadership (*see also* shared; distributed; collectivistic leadership) 6, 83-85

collectivistic leadership (*see also* shared, distributed, collective) 80-84

competencies / competency based leadership (*see also* skills) 3, 5, 8, 13, 14, 103-108

contingency leadership / theories 30-33, 37-39

Covid-19 (*see also* pandemic) 14, 15, 67, 93-94, 159, 170

criticisms of leadership studies 8-9, 53, 56, 103, 136

cultural capital (*see also* social capital) 143

CV 16-18

definition, leadership 6-8

democratic leadership (*see also* Theory X and Y) 14, 34, 35-36,

destination Marketing Organisation (DMO) 2, 51, 57-59

diversity (*see also* equality; inclusion) 141-142

distributed leadership (*see also* shared; collectivistic; collective leadership) 80-84, 87

EMBOK 19, 105

emotional intelligence competencies (*see also* LDQ; competencies) 108

employment practices (*see also* workforce) 16-18, 165-167

entity approach (*see also* trait theory; great man; behaviour; contingency; Theory X and Y) 8, 23-24, 44-45, 56, 80, 85

entity-relational approach (*see also* charismatic; transactional; transformational; LMX leadership) 44-45

entrepreneur 38-41

entrepreneurial (*see also* entrepreneur) 2, 39, 41, 129

equality (*see also* diversity; inclusion) 141-142; 154, 159 ethical leadership (*see also* authentic leadership) 5, 64-70, 73, 165

event communities 129, 137, 142-145

event competencies 105-109

expert power (*see also* coercive power, legitimate power, reward power, referent power) 140, 159

explicit knowledge (*see also* tacit knowledge; implicit knowledge; latent knowledge) 117, 119-120, 122, 126, 130

festivals 2, 26, 28, 67, 115, 128, 157, 161-163

Fielder's theory of leadership 31-33

followers (*see also* followship) 5, 8, 31, 32, 44-48, 50, 52, 54, 56, 66, 69, 70, 136, 18

followship (*see also* followers) 52, 91

global challenges / consciousness 15, 82, 104, 141, 144, 153-155, 159

graduates 16

great man (*see also* trait theory; entity approaches; heroic leadership) 4, 24-26, 46

heroic leadership (*see also* great man; charismatic; post heroic) 5, 26-27, 44-46, 56, 80, 94

Hersey & Blanchard's situational theory 33

history, of leadership 4-6

implicit knowledge (*see also* latent knowledge; explicit knowledge; tacit knowledge) 122-123, 127, 130

inclusion (*see also* equality, diversity) 141-142

influence 7, 26, 31, 35, 48, 53, 75, 80, 82, 85, 90, 109-111, 138, 141, 145

intellectual competencies (*see also* LDQ; competencies) 108

knowledge
aspects of 118-122
value of 116-118

knowledge management (*see also* tacit knowledge) 118, 123-130

laissez faire leadership (*see also* authoritarian leadership; democratic leadership) 34, 35-36

latent knowledge (see implicit knowledge; explicit knowledge; tacit knowledge) 122-123, 127, 130

LDQ model 107-108

Leader Member Exchange (LMX) 53-56, 59, 66

leaderless events 163-165

leadership
definition 6-8
in event literature 12-14
styles 3, 13, 14, 28, 30, 33-36, 45, 51, 54, 56, 74-76

Leadmill 167-169

legitimate power (*see also* coercive power; reward power; expert power; referent power) 140, 145

LMX (Leader Member Exchange) 53-56, 59, 66

management 7, 74-75

managerial competencies (*see also* LDQ; competencies) 7, 108

MBECS (*see also* competencies; skills) 19, 104, 105-108, 111

Index

moral leadership (*see also* new wave) 5, 64-73, 76
motivation 32-33, 47-50, 55, 140

new wave (of leadership studies) (*see also* moral leadership; ethical leadership; servant leadership; authentic leadership) 5, 64-73, 76

pandemic (*see also* Covid-19) 14, 15, 67, 93-94, 159, 170
Path-Goal theory 32
personality (*see also* trait / great man) 24-26, 28-29, 30, 37, 116
post-heroic (*see also* heroic) 5, 45, 56
power (*see also* coercive power, reward power, expert power, referent power, legitimate power) 85, 126, 128, 136-149
psychometric testing 26, 28, 37, 41

referent power (*see also* coercive power, legitimate power, reward power, expert power) 140
relational leadership (*see also* followers; followship, charismatic leadership; transactional leadership; transformational leadership) 5, 8, 44-46, 69, 81
reward power (*see also* coercive power, legitimate power, expert power, referent power) 140

servant leadership 5, 8, 65, 70-73, 76
shared leadership (*see also* distributed leadership; collective leadership; collectivistic leadership) 80-84; 84-88, 92, 94

shared identity (*see also* social identity theory) 89-91
skills (*see also* competencies) 10, 13, 14, 103-111, 117, 147, 165
situational leadership (*see also* contingency leadership; Hersey & Blanchard's situational theory) 25, 30-33, 37, 51
Social Agents of Change 151-165
social capital (*see also* cultural capital) 143
social identity theory (*see also* shared identity) 89-91
stakeholders / stakeholder management 11, 28, 70, 110, 128, 145-146

tacit knowledge (*see also* knowledge management; explicit knowledge; implicit knowledge; latent knowledge) 117, 119-120, 122-133
team leadership 87-89, 92
Theory X and Theory Y 33-36
trait theory (*see also* great man) 5, 24-29, 31, 37, 41, 46, 102, 104
transactional leadership (*see also* transformational leadership) 45, 47-52, 59
transformational leadership (*see also* transactional leadership) 45, 47-52, 59
trust 3, 39, 50, 54, 66, 69, 71, 86, 89, 94

unique industry setting 10, 15, 36

vertical leadership 84, 87, 137
vision 7, 11, 12, 27, 41, 50, 53, 57-59, 121

workforce (*see also* employment practices) 14-16

www.ingramcontent.com/pod-product-compliance
Ingram Content Group UK Ltd.
Pitfield, Milton Keynes, MK11 3LW, UK
UKHW021555180525
458674UK00014B/83